too fast to live

too fast to live
valerio viccei

BLAKE

Published by Blake Publishing Ltd,
3, Bramber Court
2 Bramber Road
London W14 9PB

First published in Great Britain in 2000

ISBN 185782 411 3

All rights reserved. No part of this publication may be reproduced, stored in a retrieval system, or in any form or by any means, without the prior permission in writing of the publisher, nor be otherwise circulated in any form of binding or cover other than that in which it is published and without a similar condition including this condition being imposed on the subsequent purchaser.

British Library Cataloguing-in-Publication Data: A catalogue record for this book is available from the British Library.

Typeset by Jon Davies

Printed by CPD Wales

1 3 5 7 9 10 8 6 4 2

©Text copyright Valerio Viccei

I dedicate this book to my Mother and Father,
to my sister Raffa, my brother Paolo
and also to Gianni and Helle. I don't know
if I am rightfully worthy of their unshakeable love,
but they are the six people who really matter to me.

Contents

	Acknowledgements	ix
	Prologue	xvii
	Introduction	xxiii
1	The Shock of My Life	1
2	A Shark in a Fishpond	9
3	Back on My Feet	69
4	Almost in the Bag	87
5	The 'Key' to the Vaults	115
6	Down to Business	127
7	The Eternal Triangle	165
8	The Final Stage	181
9	Like Watching a Movie	213
10	Aladdin's Cave	245
11	London, a Month Later	275
	Aftermath	283

Acknowledgements

Writing a book is a complex matter by any standards; it requires an awful lot of patience, dedication and resources. Writing a book in prison, in the most secure unit in the country, does not make things any easier and there have been times when even my firm commitment has been on the verge of collapsing.

Prison is a very peculiar environment and men with the most varied of backgrounds, political beliefs, and attitudes to captivity have to live extremely close to one another. Then, you have the prison officers, the various governors, the probation/education and medical staff. A colourful, and sometimes very volatile mix, with which I have learned to come to terms. Some of these people, as in every other walk of life, are a terrible pain in the ass and I'm not going to spend many words over them. I can only say that prisoners do not need further aggravation from staff who are bitter, frustrated and deeply resentful. We are paying what society calls a heavy 'debt' and the only punishment we have to endure consists of deprivation of our freedom. This does not imply humiliation, loss of dignity and personality, but some officers, especially in London jails, are very dedicated to the task of making sure that inmates become numbers and are denied basic rights. This is shameful and dead wrong.

Personally, I have been lucky somehow, as all I know are special security units and life in here is, ironically, more bearable than in most nicks: staff can't afford to be too confrontational and abuses are almost unknown. There is room for huge improvement, of course, and things seem to finally move in the right direction, although very slowly. Privatisation may be one of the answers, but employment of liberal-minded governors and the dismantling of the actual POA structure are the basic requirements for true change and a more realistic approach at the turn of the millennium.

People's perceptions about prison life are very unreal and whereas some are prone to believe that it is pure hell, some maintain it is too soft and totally inadequate for our sins. The truth, as usual, has to be found in the middle and everybody should realise that conditions vary hugely from one prison to another.

I have spent the last three years in H.M.P. Parkhurst, Isle of Wight: I am still in its Unit and from here, shortly, I will be transferred to my native Italy where I will serve the remainder of my sentence and face many other charges.

I never expected an English prison to be as good as this, and I am saying so in all honesty. Parkhurst is a one-off and its governor, John Marriott, is a one-off as well. The man has earned my respect and my appreciation; he has struggled and is still struggling in order to overcome diffidence by prisoners and opposition by the staff. He

too fast to live

has made Parkhurst a much better place and his approach is the right one. I am grateful to him for having made sure that even this little Unit, forgotten for years, had access to civil staff and teachers. I could have hardly managed to progress with this work, were it not for the Education Dept. and some of its very understanding, capable and patient teachers. I should not forget a particularly good and kind man whom I have literally pestered with my repeated requests concerning typewriters, word processors and similar contraptions: he's no teacher, but one of the assistant Governors and his name is Louis Simpson. He has run this Unit, during his term, like a true gentleman and has always managed to find the right balance in order to satisfy both security and little, but precious improvements. Another man who has made the difference is Kevin Rogers, the Deputy Governor. He is a genuine and intelligent person, one who runs the show efficiently and without hesitation, easily compensating for many of his colleagues' ineffectiveness.

I have written this book all by myself and only at the very beginning did I attempt to write in Italian in order to have it translated into English. A couple of chapters were enough to make me realise that too much of its flavour would be lost, but Mrs Sandler did a beautiful job nevertheless and always encouraged me to carry on with the project. Another outstanding character to whom I owe a lot is Jim Nicholson, a friend who has been supportive all along and has kicked my ass whenever I was losing heart and about to quit the huge task parading before my very eyes. A loud thank you also to Rosie Ries, the lovely and resourceful assistant of my publisher. She is a lady of whom I am very fond and one who has worked hard for this project to materialise.

Of the various teachers who helped to transform this Italian bank robber, who three years ago could hardly put together a greetings card, into someone who has been awarded a Certificate of Proficiency in English by the Cambridge University, I want to mention Shirley. She has been and still is more than simply a teacher; she, like Jim, has been repeatedly 'kicking' me all along and never gave me the chance to even consider quitting. Her moral support has been far-reaching as much as her teaching.

Carol and Frances have also helped me to develop my command of the language and have had to put up with my incorrigible, but always friendly chauvinism. They hit back all right, with the result that stimulating teaching has delivered huge improvement.

A word also for James, of Technical Support Services, whose expertise and extensive knowledge of computers, printers and word processors has been priceless to me. With him goes Iain, another computer wizard whom I drove mad, and by whom I was often driven insane. Of all I must not forget Don Swinton, the prison senior psychologist and a man whom I deeply respect. He has kept me together when my father was seriously ill and about to go. Like all big men, only then did I realise how small and vulnerable I am if confronted with tragedies of such magnitude. Don's tactfulness, intelligence and genuine friendship saw me through the worst period of

too fast to live

my entire life. You don't forget these things and mine is just a little way to show my appreciation to him. Thanks Don.

A word for the best of all my English solicitors, Clive Wiggins. One for 'Fred' Richard Leach, who is the closest thing to a fair cop and one for Colin Nott, who was there when I needed him. One even for His Lordship Robert Lymbery, who sentenced me to 22 years but, in the aftermath of the trial, proved to be balanced and professional, sparing a good word for my repatriation to Italy. Sir Antony and Lady Bienvenida Buck did the same: she, in particular, is a good friend whose loyalty has not wavered regardless of every possible embarrassment and criticism.

A tribute is also due to Fabio Marini and Paola Pedicone, my efficient Italian lawyers, whose professionalism and tenacity made sure that I survived so many legal battles although detained abroad and have never let me down. I must not forget all my relatives without distinction, my friends Umberto, Mauro, Felice, Miro, Piero, Rolando, Angelo, Daniela, Sandra, Karen, Tina, Renate, Martine, Kathy, Debbie, Vivienne, Lyn and Rory, Doreen, Pam and Connie and Paul, Mary A., Steve Briscoe, Julie, Larry and Paula, the Connellan clan, Carmelo and Ada, Jim D. and hundreds of other friends, pen-pals and correspondence chess players who have supported me all along.

I should also mention many Parkhurst prison officers who have been friendly, supportive and kind to me particularly when my father's illness struck. They are too

valerio viccei

numerous and it would be embarrassing to them if I would mention their full names, but 'Smarting', Derek and Linda, Alec, John R., Finlay, 'Big Tony', Ken 'the shooter', Nick, Robo, Ron, Geoff, Ken Young, even John 'the pipe' and Chris from the 'mob-squad', can all pride themselves on being good men who happen to work for the Prison Service. This familiarity may appear strange to many people and to most of the inmates, I believe, but in such a microscopic environment of a few square yards, where the officer–prisoner ratio is often three to one, we live extremely close and must learn to evaluate each other very quickly.

I have left to the end the people with whom I have closely shared the last five years: category A inmates. I met very outstanding guys: the most gentlemanly of them all is Brian Robinson, 'The Colonel'. Brian has managed to make me review my opinion about English inmates: he is a nice, organised and clever man, one who is coping with prison life with uncommon dignity and self-respect. There is also Harry, a stubborn old fellow who is best known to everybody as Big H. Among other things, he has taught me how to play chess and he has always behaved as an old-fashioned gentleman, preventing me from blowing my top on many occasions. Whatever people may think of him, a deep sense of loyalty obliges me to openly attest that I consider him a true friend. A special word for Micky Peterson, a friend with a heart of gold and extremely unlucky. Driven insane by useless prison medical staff in the seventies, he is still treated simply as a disruptive prisoner, instead of someone who

too fast to live

needs help and proper treatment. Recently, here in Parkhurst, he was repeatedly stabbed while surrounded by people whom he trusted and were allegedly his friends. Whoever was there and let it happen should explain to him why such a thing was necessary. Wayne Hurren is, together with David 'the Rhodesian', one of my best pals ever: they are two true and very lethal wolves. I will miss them badly.

There is also Eric, a partner like him makes up for all my disappointments. Finally, a word on behalf of the Alfa-male Arctic wolf, the noblest and most clever of all predators. One also for womankind, all of them without distinction, because women are what I love most.

Valerio Viccei
HMP Parkhurst, October 1992

Prologue

by James Nicholson, Britain's Most Celebrated Crime Reporter

> *'I have lived by the gun,
> and maybe one day I'll die by the gun!'*

Prophetic words from Valerio Viccei, who was shot dead on 18 April 2000, having been shadowed in his car by a squad of armed police officers.

He died under a hail of bullets which ripped into him from his groin to his head, killing him instantly. The other passenger in the car — long-standing friend, renowned armed robber and Mob boss Antonio D — was also shot and wounded.

Next to Valerio was his Magnum .357 hand-gun and spent cartridges. Not too far away was a rapid-firing M12 machine-gun. Its owner, 40-year-old Enzo Baldini, a police officer of the Italian Carabinieri, lay wounded, writhing on the ground — he would later recover after hospitalisation. The officer had been shot in the stomach, it is claimed, after a confrontation with Italy's most famous armed robber.

Valerio Viccei will go down in the annals of crime as the mastermind of the world's biggest-ever heist. No other robber, even in the crime-ridden USA, has matched his massive Knightsbridge haul, which the police say could have amounted to £40 million. Valerio claimed it was nearer £60 million. Only £10 million has been recovered.

Several questions remain unanswered: Why was Valerio's car ambushed by an armed police patrol? Who fired the first shot? Why was he travelling in a car with a gun in his possession? And what part did Antonio D have to play in this?

One major theory is that the police shot the wrong man — the Mafia man was said to be on their hit list. Another is that the undeclared war which existed between Valerio and the local police before he fled from Italy over ten years earlier, had been revived. They wanted him out of the way.

Speculation was rife in the Italian press after the shooting. It was claimed that Valerio and his pal were about to pull off a major robbery, and that their target was a farmhouse with priceless antiques. Then there was a bizarre report that Valerio had teamed up with the Mafia to kidnap a high-ranking government official and hold him to ransom.

On his own admission to me, Valerio had been a thorn in the side of the Italian police for years. They were frustrated by the large number of successful bank raids he was known to have carried out. He had been charged with raids on 15 banks, but he has admitted to having been involved in twice

too fast to live

that number. Waving a gun, he fled from the Italian courthouse with those charges, and a possible 15–30-year jail sentence, hanging over him. His next stop was London.

But Valerio had other powerful enemies. He had told friends that, among the safety deposit boxes he robbed in Knightsbridge, were two owned by notorious Mafia gangsters, linked with the collapsed Vatican bank. Huge sums of money and quantities of drugs were contained in the boxes.

Guns had always been a way of life for him. No one knew better than Valerio the risks he took going around with a blonde in one hand a gun in the other, and it was the deaths of close friends who lived similar lifestyles that prompted Valerio to tell me years later in Parkhurst, 'You know that I am fascinated with guns. When I was in Italy I felt undressed without them.' Then he added, pathetically, his prophecy: 'One day I may die by the gun.'

Valerio argued that he needed to carry weapons for his own protection. He claimed he had many enemies in Italian law enforcement agencies as well as criminals from rival gangs in Italy, and they did not take kindly to him eliminating at least one of their number, ten years before the Knightsbridge robbery.

Telling me about this shooting, Valerio said, 'I was alerted that this guy was looking for me with a gun. I found him first and he became history. I had no option. If I had not taken him out, I would not be here today. My friends disposed of his body.'

Valerio's Knightsbridge robbery won him many enemies here

in the UK. Among them were high-profile villains and drugs barons who were among the 30 people who did not come forward after the robbery to say that their boxes had been plundered.

Valerio later confirmed that kilos of cocaine worth a fortune were found and, according to him, quickly disposed of! Unused Vatican passports and bundles of money and documents said to be connected to Italian banker Roberto Calvi were also hidden away in a box.

Valerio was interviewed by the police about this but refused to talk about the documents or the money for fear of reprisals when he returned to Italy. He knew the money belonged to the Mafia. No doubt some of it is still hidden away in another safety deposit box and only Valerio knows — knew — the box number. It is doubtful whether Valerio ever trusted anyone with the numbers or location of the boxes.

The police realise, too, that he had plenty of time to hide his spoils. And while he was alive, money seemed no object. He drove a Ferrari, and sported a £20,000 gold necklace and a glittering £10,000 gold Rolex diamond oyster watch, thanks to his successful armed raid on Coutts' bank.

Life was good. By his own admission he was sitting on millions. And that is one reason why it is difficult for me to accept that the night he was shot dead he was planning another heist — he simply did not need the money.

And his death leaves another riddle: 'Where is the money?' I once asked him naïvely.

Valerio smiled, touched the end of his nose, and winked.

too fast to live

'Don't forget, I had plenty of time to dispose of the loot. Think about London, and the trips I made to South America, Israel, Paris and Belgium before I was caught. Yes, I had it all planned out in case they did catch up with me.'

I spent countless hours with Valerio when he was writing this book in Parkhurst. He sought my advice on several topics that he could not include in his book because he still had to face outstanding charges in Italy.

He also discussed at length his many love affairs. One, he confided, was a titled lady, another a small-part film actress. But he did not write about them because he wanted to protect their identities.

His real love was for Helle Scoubon, the Danish beauty and London fashion shop manageress to whom this book is partly dedicated. She is now back in Copenhagen, shattered by the news of his death and manner of his passing.

She was present at his funeral in his home town of Ascoli Pinceno, which was attended only by his family. Helle wept when she saw his body, saying, 'He was shot many times ... and we don't know why. The family are devastated. They have been told nothing. People in Italy are suspicious about the shooting. They are saying it was a "set-up". They are not being told why the car was stopped or who fired first. Reports were put out that he was shot 28 times. This is not true. His own doctor attended the autopsy and says he was shot eight times. It is so distressing for the family whose questions have remained unanswered.

'We are waiting now to hear from Valerio's friend who was also hurt in the police ambush. Perhaps he can tell us what really happened that night.'

Detective Inspector Dick Leach, a fine police officer and the man who arrested Valerio for the Knightsbridge raid visited him in Italy shortly before his death. After the shooting Dick told me: 'I cannot condone the use of guns in any shape or form, and to hear that a policeman was shot shocks me. Valerio promised me that he had put all that behind him and was looking forward to an early release. We all know he was sitting on a mountain of money and he could retire a millionaire.

'So it baffles me to think he was out on another heist. It looks very suspicious ... almost like a set-up. I am aware of what happened to one or two of his friends, who were killed in a similar fashion. Valerio had made a lot of enemies in high places and we know he was not well loved by some of my counterparts in Italy.

'Whoever shot whom, Valerio should not have been carrying a gun or accompanying another villain. I am sorry to learn of his death. I spoke to him on the telephone only three days before the shooting and had arranged to see him in Italy in June.

'He lived a dangerous life ... and in the end, sadly, he met a violent death.'

As I write, the questions remain unanswered and the wounded Mafia man has not been charged. Meanwhile, the police here in London would also like their questions answered. Where are the missing millions?

The Old Bailey, July 2000

Introduction

Central Criminal Court, 30 January 1989

'The stakes were colossal. Having lost you have to pay the price accordingly. In this court I have seen a man of charm and courtesy, a man of substantial abilities. But these qualities combined with others serve to make you a very dangerous man . . . therefore I sentence you to twenty-two years imprisonment.'

These were the words spoken by Judge Robert Lymbery while sentencing Valerio Viccei, after he was found guilty by unanimous verdict, of one of the most daring robberies of the twentieth century.

The Italian listened carefully, nodded and then shrugged his shoulders. He also lightly squeezed his interpreter's hand as if to say that everything was fine. He cracked jokes with the press and his heavy escort until he was led away.

Both the police investigation and the trial itself had failed to discover how many people participated in the Knightsbridge raid, nor were they able to trace most of the missing loot, let alone establish its true amount. Only Valerio Viccei knew everything that had happened. It was he who had planned the robbery to the minutest detail; he chose all the participants, disposed of the stolen goods and distributed the money to his accomplices. Although he stood in the witness box for many days, the Italian steadfastly refused to name the other people involved, or to give detailed information about the planning and selling phase of the robbery.

Since the day of his arrest Valerio had taken full responsibility for what happened, but he had never admitted to the robbery charge. In court he cheekily maintained that it could not have been a robbery at all if the victims themselves were accomplices, and that this was exactly what he had been told by a phantomlike 'mastermind' of the raid. To his knowledge, he said, it was all a gigantic insurance swindle. Naturally, the jury did not believe him, and rightly so. But he gave it his best shot and, in doing so, kept a lot of other people out of trouble. Although he was repeatedly warned by the judge that his reticence in answering some questions would weigh enormously against him. Valerio said that he was prepared to accept that rather than involve others.

This book is the key to all those unanswered

questions, and many more.

> *'Crime had become to me what narcotics are to a junkie:*
> *I simply could not live without it. Like heavy drugs,*
> *crime at its highest level generates the worst kind of addiction.'*
>
> Valerio Viccei

CHAPTER 1

The Shock of My Life

Coutts & Co. is probably the most exclusive bank in the Western World — after all its most distinguished client is the Queen herself! That must be the reason why none of its few branches had ever been robbed in the three centuries of the bank's existence. This record ended, however, just before Christmas 1986 when I cleaned out the Sloane Avenue branch. That operation had proved so easy that I decided to help myself to some more of Coutts' cash. I had no doubt that security would be stepped up but I knew that if only I could get a proper look around the premises of a few branches, I would be able to come up with the best plan of operation. After careful checks, I decided that the Cavendish Square branch was a suitable target.

Cavendish Square is in the very centre of London,

valerio viccei

with Piccadilly just a few hundred yards away. It is surrounded by very important buildings, the traffic is often jammed, but there are not many shops for the pedestrians to mill around. The Coutts Bank branch was a very large one and the main entrance was on the quietest side of the square. It was the perfect site for a predator's strike. The glass panels of its door were heavily tinted and there was no way that a passer-by could see anything happening inside. The ground floor was huge, but divided into many sectors and on the right there was a sort of wooden stall where a security man normally sat. There were three tellers to deal with the public and they all sat behind a counter of heavy wood supporting the usual metal frames holding reinforced glass panels. As in some other branches of Coutts, a peculiarity of this counter was that there were wide gaps which enabled face-to-face contact with the bank's exclusive clients.

A security video camera was installed above the main entrance and pointed its wide-angled lens towards the counter. I had not been able to spot any monitor in front of the security man and therefore knew the bank hall must be kept under observation by a member of staff in another room. I had gone inside a couple of times and on both occasions had exchanged sterling for dollars, an innocent transaction, giving me a good excuse to have another look at the layout and security arrangements.

No problem at all!

*   *   *

too fast to live

Early on the afternoon of a cold day in January 1987, I revved up the powerful engine of a 650cc GPZ Kawasaki which I had stolen two months earlier in Camden Town. My partner sat on the pillion. We were both wearing bikers' gear under which we had hidden a sawn-off shotgun and a semi-automatic pistol. After a couple of reconnaissance trips around the square and the nearby backstreets, I dropped my partner off so that he could cover the last thirty yards to the bank on foot. I parked the bike just outside the main entrance and, after a further discreet survey of the surroundings, I went inside, followed by my colleague.

As soon as I got in I nearly swore out loud — there were at least five customers queuing up in front of the two operating tills; the third cashier must have gone out for lunch in the way they do when things get busy. People do not bother me, but their unpredictability often complicates matters beyond belief. On top of that, my partner would be the one who had to deal with them while I worked on the other side of the counter. I was beginning to have a bad feeling about this but bank robbing is no business for pussycats and I never waver in a crisis, even though in my country the security man, and probably at least two of the customers, would have been carrying guns. That notwithstanding, I have never walked out on a bank raid because of the possible risks: it is nasty work, but you must think of it as though you were a surgeon and put aside all emotions and feelings.

I stood at the back of one of the two queues with my partner right behind me. If anybody got suspicious of two

valerio viccei

men wearing full-face crash helmets and gloves, I could hardly blame them. I was soon feeling impatient and was not prepared to wait much longer, well aware that my partner might lose his bottle and walk out (after all, he was not Italian!), so I shoved aside a well-dressed, pompous gentleman and reached for my handgun at the same time. So far I had said nothing and the man was outraged by my behaviour; he barked something about waiting my turn in a tone that was typical of someone used to issuing orders to working class people. To him I was just a messenger who had invaded the privacy and the exclusivity of his posh bank. Once his arrogance subsided enough for him to notice my gun, however, he soon went quiet and shock took the place of outrage. The other customers were quicker than him and more realistic; they calmly made room for me and complied with my request to lie down on the floor.

Of course, all of this happened at lightning speed and the cashiers hardly had time to understand what was going on. I landed on the counter with a single jump and motioned to one of the cashiers to get off her stool and move towards the wall. I did not want to harm anybody; my only aim was to get the money. The other cashier was quick to obey, but this silly girl hesitated, causing quite a problem because if she did not move from her chair I couldn't get through the gap!

I was experienced enough in these situations to realise that she might be reacting that way through shock, so I was not going to be nasty, but at the same time I had to do something as whoever was watching the monitor

too fast to live

would already have hit the 'red' button and the police would be on their way. I raised my voice and she jumped like a scared rabbit. 'Fine!' I told her as she began to pull a bank note from the till. Now I moved on, hurling myself over the counter. The whole scene was very calm.

As I filled the bag with the till's contents, a deafening noise erupted, making me jump. Oh no! The shotgun must have gone off!

When I lifted my eyes above the counter I was so shocked that I could not at first take in what had happened. Thick stainless steel panels had risen from the massive counter and, driven by a powerful compressor, had hit the ceiling of their frames with a loud bang. While the shields remained in position they would prevent me from getting out or communicating with my partner.

This situation was extremely dangerous for all of us. I had not expected a thing like that to happen — ever — and therefore had not planned a possible way out in advance. I could hear my partner yelling on the other side and then, for a fraction of a second, the shields came down and up again. I have never trusted this sort of gadget and realised that if I tried to get out the same way I got in, the bloody thing could easily rip off one of my arms or crush my rib cage.

I began to yell at the girl who had pulled the note from the till, activating a hidden device. I told her that doing such a thing was totally dumb. The system was supposed to keep me out, but instead I was now locked in with her and she'd better find a quick way to let me

valerio viccei

out or we would all be in serious trouble. She probably realized her big mistake, but just lay on the floor motionless. I am not a nasty man, so I turned to the other girl who seemed more sensible. I lowered my voice and quietly told her to get me out of there immediately because once the police arrived she would be taken hostage and that was gonna be bad! She got up quickly and began to fiddle with a panel full of switches and bright little lights. It was the alarm control system and I hoped she knew what she was doing. The shields came down again, then suddenly exploded towards the ceiling with frightening force. The girl looked at me, genuinely puzzled: 'I don't know what's happening: they should stay down.' I realised that the bastard in front of the monitor was playing games with both the customers' and his colleagues' lives, let alone my freedom, but my main priority was to get out as soon as possible. During one of the 'tricks' played by the metal shields I had observed the other side; and everything seemed to be under my partner's control — no panic and no police either!

To my left there was a door which I had already tried to open. It appeared to be locked and I considered the possibility that it was connected to the shield system. The next time they came down, I rushed for the door handle and wrenched it open. It worked! The shield came down and stayed down.

For a fraction of a second I stared at my partner who could hardly believe it was me. He shouted that we must leave immediately. I had to admire his courage. He could have taken off at any time and left me in deep shit while the customers ran out hysterically.

Although I was worried and still tense, I had not yet left the cashiers' room. By blocking the door with my right foot I prevented it from locking itself while I thought intently. With the characteristic unpredictability that has often driven my partners insane, I grabbed a chair which I put between the door and its frame. My partner started to swear at me but I shouted back that we had come to get money, not to shoot a movie, and money we would get. I walked back into the room and started to fill my large nylon rucksack with bundles of cash, but I had little time to waste and had to leave some in the tills and in a little safe.

Finally I removed the chair and walked into the hall of the bank which was deadly quiet. I did not rush and the photos produced by the prosecution during my later trial show that I even stopped to replace the gun in one of my breast pockets. My partner was on the brink of a breakdown and I was afraid he might even shoot me, so I placed the rucksack on his shoulders saying that everything was fine. We had done it!

This may be what I said, but I knew that only when we walked out of the bank would we find out the truth. I might have replaced my gun too early. On the other hand, if things were fine I couldn't afford to walk out on the pavement gun in hand. I checked outside through a large window but I could see nothing amiss. The traffic was regular and a couple of pedestrians were walking towards the bank. Had the police already been there, the

valerio viccei

area would have been sealed off and the public forbidden to come too close.

The Kawasaki engine roared as soon as I pushed the button and in a fraction of a second we had disappeared through a maze of backstreets. We reached the chosen place for the changeover and, after placing all my partner's gear in a large sports bag previously strapped to the bike seat, I got rid of my crash helmet and walked towards a Mercedes saloon with German plates. I opened its boot, slung in the sports bag and got into the car. Before I started the engine I could hear the siren of a police car. The direction of the sound indicated that the police were heading for the bank. I could smile again, but the shock was huge; I had only just made it. I could hardly recall a job where I was so close to feeling lost.

* * *

But perhaps I had better begin at the beginning . . .

CHAPTER 2

A Shark in a Fishpond

London, New Year's Day 1986

My trip from Dover to London had been quick and I managed to relax for the first time since I left Italy. Immigration control had been swift and superficial. Everybody seemed too tired from the recent Christmas and New Year celebrations to pay attention to someone like me. I was dressed inconspicuously and worked to blend with the crowd. My train arrived at Victoria, one of Europe's largest and busiest stations. Passengers spilled out on to the platform in incredible numbers and I wondered where they had all been hiding, as I hadn't noticed so many at Dover.

London hit me with a sense of sheer confusion. My

valerio viccei

ears buzzed with dozens of languages and dialects, all babbled simultaneously by a complete mix of races. The more I looked around, the more I was convinced I had just landed on another planet.

I was not just a small-town boy; in fact I had lived in Rome for many years and travelled extensively, but this was weird, I am telling you! Everywhere I looked were filthy punks with spiky orange hair standing upright on their heads as if defying the laws of gravity. There were tramps of all colours, some begging in a really pushy way, strange guys in leather clothes, wearing gloves that covered only half of their hands. Some of this mob wore tribal costumes and what would be traffic-stopping headdresses in every other European city. I tried not to forget that such sights only make an impression on tourists or newcomers like me, but I couldn't help feeling confused, nonetheless.

This so-called civilised London seemed to me no different from Paris, Rome and Amsterdam. The main difference was that whereas in each of them I would have already spotted ten uniformed, armed cops all I had seen here so far were a couple of bobbies who smiled at everybody and appeared totally to ignore the awful parade around them. Life in London would suit me just fine!

With a sad expression on my face and my luggage in my hand, I slowly tried to make my way in what looked like a modern Babylon. The fatigue of the journey and the suspense of the various frontier checks were beginning to tell on me. If only I could get to a hotel and

too fast to live

sleep for a whole week! Well, that was just wishful thinking as I knew I couldn't afford it and that I was now on enemy ground where any oversight, any small slip, could finish me off. There were things to be done, no matter how tired and low I felt.

Wrapped in these depressing thoughts, I made for one of the station exits and started looking for a phone box. Completely forgetting that I only had Italian and French coins with me, I began to fight with one of these cursed contraptions. As far as I was concerned the instructions might just as well have been printed in Chinese. I only knew enough English to buy a newspaper, anything more complicated than that was well beyond my understanding. I already hated England and felt it was all going to be even harder than I had expected.

I knew myself well enough to realise that if I didn't calm down, I would lose my temper, and considering that I had only just arrived, it was a bit too early to get carried away. 'What a bloody awful start!' I told myself, only in Italian and a little too loudly. Still wearing an expression that told it all, I managed to find a money exchange bureau. I tried to trade in all my foreign currency for 'sterling', but all the idiot of a cashier would offer me was 'pounds'.

'What the hell is that?' I asked him in a style of English that must have made him believe I was a weirdo. He ignored me and just punched the keyboard of his little calculator, then showed me numbers that had lost a lot of zeros during his obscure operations. I handed over millions of lire and the bandit gave me a few hundred pounds. I glared at him, deeply regretting the loss of my Walther pistol. It might have given me better bargaining power.

Only later did I realise that pounds and sterling are the same thing!

*   *   *

Starting twenty minutes earlier, I had dialled the same phone number three times already. Still no answer. In my frustration, I was getting very close to smashing up the telephone. A nagging suspicion had just occurred to me that perhaps that cursed Greenwich Mean Time and that typical British obstinacy in doing everything the wrong way round had conspired to alter the clock when the depressing ring of the phone was suddenly broken off by a pleasant, but rather strained female voice muttering something in English. All I could manage to say was a simple: 'A friend of Mauro's speaking.'

'Uno momento,' came the brief reply. Her Italian was no better than my English, and for the first time since leaving Italy, I managed to smile. Then it seemed that Mauro came to the phone. I could not understand what the hell was going on at the other end of the line. He babbled on in a mixture of English and Italian, talking half to me and half to the female voice I could still hear somewhere in the background. A three-way conversation started up, punctuated with squeals and reproaches in both languages. I kept quiet and listened, with my eyes closed, just agreeing with everything that was said, which

too fast to live

I completely failed to understand.

My old friend Mauro had changed a lot in the past three years — perhaps learning a new language had helped to complicate his already chaotic existence! 'What a fucking great start,' I thought again, and not for the last time either.

Mauro thought a taxi might be the best way to get to his house, but I wouldn't even hear of it and I made sure that he realised I was tired and losing my temper. I knew how risky this approach was from my previous experience of Mauro. He was quite capable of changing his mind and leaving for Scotland during those few crucial minutes and not turning up again until the middle of next week! I could see the headlines already: ITALIAN CAR DEALER MARRIED TO AN ENGLISH WOMAN IS KILLED IN A FRENZY BY A FELLOW COUNTRYMAN!

I recognised the car bearing Mauro and his wife with no difficulty. It would have been impossible to miss it — a noisy old Maserati with Italian number plates — now drawing up opposite the main entrance to Victoria Station. It only needed a little Italian flag tied to the aerial to complete the picture.

For some obscure reason Mauro introduced me to his young English wife as Gigi, and she made it quite plain that she was anything but happy about the whole thing. My instant gut reaction was to break away from them as soon as possible.

The days went by slowly but definitely not smoothly. Mauro and his wife always seemed to be at loggerheads.

valerio viccei

They fought all the time over everything. Worse still, she knew I was on the run, having wormed this out of her fool of a husband. Mauro had never been a tough guy but now he had dwindled to a shadow of his former self: feeble, irritable and ineffectual. He was typical of an Italian who had married a foreigner and now lived in her country like a silly wop. She was also pregnant, however, and this complicated things even more.

During a particularly fierce quarrel, Tilly had a bad turn and threatened to call the police. I was gripped by panic, but really couldn't blame her as by then she had a belly the size of a hot air balloon, and they had been exchanging pretty hefty blows. As soon as Mauro left the apartment, braying like the ass he was, I took her to the nearest casualty department, which happened to be in the Fulham Road, just round the corner from where we were staying.

I sat there with her, sweating. I had no idea how things worked in this bloody country, but I had already learned enough to know that women were running it and that if Tilly was going to make too big a deal out of this little quarrel, I was in deep shit. I didn't even know if they had uniformed police at the hospital reception desk, as they do in Italy, so I told Tilly to stay on the bench while I went to find help on her behalf. I did exactly that, and when at last one of the nurses managed to understand what I was muttering about, I asked her to hold on for a second as I had got my car parked right outside the entrance!

Actually there was no car and as soon as I left the

too fast to live

reception area my legs picked up speed at an incredible rate.

I decided that I had had enough of these two lunatics and would rather face the unknown than end up getting lifted by the police for a domestic quarrel that had nothing to do with me. The next day I rented a flat in North London and another important chapter of my life began.

*   *   *

I enrolled for an advanced course in English and explored the city centre for several weeks. Going back to school at the age of thirty, surrounded by au pairs and secretaries-to-be, proved a very hard task even by my own standards. I hated sitting in a classroom for hours and was unable to concentrate on anything. I often found myself dozing off or totally immersed in my own thoughts, with the result that I learned very little while greatly annoying the teacher.

Obviously I was using a phoney name — Pierluigi something — but as this was an entirely new identity I did not think of myself as Pierluigi something. During one lesson, while concentrating on my plans for the future and totally absorbed by this, I suddenly discovered that I was being watched by all the students. For a second I thought I had dozed off and began to apologise but was interrupted by the teacher himself who addressed me very politely: 'Pierluigi, are you feeling all right?'

'Yes, sure, the fact is that I am very tired and . . .'

'I understand that, but you were not asleep, your eyes were wide open! I have been calling your name repeatedly to no avail. Is anything wrong with your hearing? Please, do not feel embarrassed to tell me.'

How could I tell this poor man that my name was not Pierluigi something and that, as far as I was concerned, he could have shouted it in Esperanto. This was pretty embarrassing. I couldn't even say that my hearing was faulty when, for over two weeks, it had been perfect.

'Well, I apologise, mister, but when I was a kid I had a very bad car crash and seriously hurt my head. Since then I tend to black out from time to time and when it happens it is as though I am lobotomised.' I said this almost biting my tongue and not looking at the poor bastard just to prevent myself from exploding into laughter, with the result that I managed to look really embarrassed.

The teacher couldn't stop apologising and the atmosphere in the classroom became a little tense for everybody. Needless to say that was the last time I set foot in the school.

*   *   *

My new retreat proved to be the best investment I ever made. I gradually began to make new contacts and to regain my confidence but, best of all, I could entertain female company for the first time since my departure from Italy.

After a couple of months I moved to another flat. It

too fast to live

was in a smart area of Chelsea, a wealthy, fashionable neighbourhood close to the Thames. I found out about the flat through an Italian friend of mine and, in fact, we had been looking for a place to share. He would be spending only a few weeks a year in England, nevertheless he wanted a nice base. This suited me fine. My landlady was Swedish, a former model by the name of Susan. She was young, smart and good looking. Many years of London life had left her relatively unscathed, but she had decided to go back to Sweden. She was feeling lonely and had probably had enough of the rain.

When I first met Susan I was quite impressed, but my command of the language was still so poor that I felt too embarrassed to speak and let my friend do all the talking. Women are a strange lot and, in my case, they often misinterpret my attitude. She did so on this occasion and thought I was shy!

My friend, whose name was Sandro, reached an agreement with her and the flat was rented for six months, starting from the week ahead. Soon after the contract was signed, we decided to celebrate with a night out together.

Sandro organised everything, and as I knew him well, I could bet he would try to bring some cocaine with him.

I was OK about the set-up, but a little pissed off at the fact that Sandro was bringing along an English girl who didn't speak Italian, while from the little I had discovered, Susan couldn't speak a word of it either. I felt I was going to look a real dummy.

valerio viccei

It was a good guess and I brooded like a spoiled kid the whole time we spent at the table of the French restaurant. I would have liked to tell Susan that it was a shame we couldn't communicate properly and that I would love to take her to bed there and then, but there was no way I could put together all that without looking like a stuttering jerk. I gave it up.

After a lovely meal and a few glasses of champagne, that knocked a huge hole in my troubled finances, the four of us finally rose and decided to head for Susan's flat. Don't ask me how, but in the few hundred yards separating the restaurant from the flat, Sandro managed to convince Susan to tell him where he could buy a few grams of good cocaine. The man was mad: here we were, her tenants to be, asking her where we could get some snow.

Susan didn't seem to mind at all and for once I was glad that she thought I couldn't understand much English as I felt like a shit. I imagined that she must think we were a couple of junkies, but it was worse than that — as I discovered later — in fact she thought we were both queer. Arghhhhhh!

As usual, the cocaine hunt went on for a while and I was getting fed up with the whole thing. At one point, while Sandro and Susan had gone God knows where, I was left sitting in the car with this totally dumb and humourless girl who, I felt, wouldn't mind having sexual intercourse there and then.

I had met her on a couple of previous occasions: once when I was with an Italian girlfriend from Ascoli, while

too fast to live

on the other I was with a totally pissed bimbo who kept trying to unzip my trousers during a party.

Now this girl asked if I was already sleeping with Susan. I said that I wished I was, adding that, as far as I was concerned, I would not mind having sex with her as well! I rather hoped that this would shut her up but she started laughing and said that she knew that already.

I decided that she was not perhaps as dumb as I had thought in the first place and, giving her a more attentive look, I realised that she was not bad at all. I knew that Sandro was not too interested in sex, so if she stayed with me she might end up having the time of her life. I would definitely ask him if he minded me making the young lady happy. To my knowledge they were just good friends anyway.

She came a little closer, but rather put me off balance when she said: 'I have seen you on three occasions, and each time you were with a different girl. You are a pig!'

I had not expected this and tried to think of a good reply. 'That's correct, darling, and that's why you want to find out how a sexist pig can make a smart girl like you scream with pleasure, am I right?'

'You are an arrogant pig and a chauvinistic bastard!'

'Look, kid, if we are going to argue, you had better choose simpler words or I won't be able to understand what you say.'

'Fuck off. Do you understand that?' she said very slowly.

I started laughing and she laughed too, punching me lightly on the shoulder. I knew that even if I failed to communicate with Susan, I still wouldn't end up on my own. Sandro would be quite happy with his cocaine.

When they returned Susan and Sandro were both smiling, thank God, which meant they had found what they were looking for and we could finally go home.

In a short while we were at Susan's place and none of us minded having a good line of what looked like decent gear by London standards. I hadn't had a line of cocaine in years; the last was while I was in prison in Italy. I wondered how I was going to feel. The unmistakable effect of this 'party' was that a new bond now existed between us and we were all at ease. Cocaine is a very individual drug and each of us was definitely thinking how to exploit it to his, or her, best advantage.

Sandro was his usual self and a little too greedy; he disappeared into the loo for a while and I knew he was already stuffing his nose, with the result that he was the first to get lost in his own thoughts. He soon got entangled in a philosophical discussion with 'bubblehead', who kept dipping the filter of her cigarette in a little tray of cocaine and glancing at me from time to time. I was struggling to communicate with Susan. Like all foreigners, I found it much easier to talk to another foreigner than to a native. We spoke slowly and always assumed the other party did not understand what we had said. 'I am doing fine,' I thought.

Susan was bright and easy going, but I was taking risks here as the other girl was clearly becoming irritated whenever we laughed aloud or touched each other. I felt sorry that I would have to tell Susan a lot of bullshit

too fast to live

about myself, but what else could I do? I am a born predator; one of the most successful bank robbers in a tough country like Italy, a man who had made adventure, sex and self-sufficiency his life's goals, and here I was, telling this nice girl that I was a dumb motor-sport reporter, who was studying English and living on his family's money. I felt like a heel again as I told her I was the kind of person I have always hated. She seemed not to mind, but I definitely did.

Time went fast and at 3 am we called it a day. Completely off his head, Sandro decided that he could drive his friend home, at which point she looked at me as if to suggest a different proposal, but she had become too chatty and I couldn't stand it. Besides I was not going to drive, or be driven by Sandro, at that time of day. I told them they could go by car if they wanted to, but I was going to catch a cab. Of the two, the girl seemed to be the one who resented it more. As soon as she turned round to grab her handbag in order to leave, I started pulling faces behind her back. Susan could hardly suppress her laughter and, as I was about to get up from the sofa, she gently pushed me back and said: 'There's the phone for the cab, but if you don't mind sleeping on the sofa, you can stay here. Besides, from next week this will be your flat. Anyway, I leave it up to you.'

I was a bit confused at this and all I managed to say was that I appreciated her kindness but did not want to seem like an intruder. I added that this hadn't been planned at all and that it was still her flat, not mine. She looked at me and smiled, disappeared into her bedroom

valerio viccei

and, even before Sandro and bubblehead had shut the door, she was back with a pillow and some blankets.

Oh God! This is going to be the most embarrassing night of my life: full of cocaine and with a pretty lady sleeping only five yards away from me!

Susan spent some time in the bathroom and then, after cleaning up the mess in the living room, she gave me a little kiss on the cheek and said good night. She walked into her bedroom but did not shut the door completely!

I had never been in a position like this in my whole life and I did not know what to do. The main problem was that I couldn't express myself as I would like to and if I made the wrong move I would end up in deep shit. While I was still desperately thinking of something to say, which is always the worst part even in your own language and especially when a total stranger is concerned, she solved all my problems with a simple, 'Gigi, if it is too cold there, or the sofa is too small for you, you can sleep here with me. I don't mind.'

My luck was in! 'Thank you,' I called loudly, but I did not just leap up and rush in there. I decided to take my time.

Women are a lovely and strange lot; that's why she must have misinterpreted my delay in accepting her warm proposal. When I walked into her room she had turned the other way and was feigning deep sleep. But you can't sleep after snorting coke for three hours, can you?

I was wearing nothing and, as soon as I lifted the

too fast to live

sheets, I found that she was naked too. She was a natural redhead and her skin was very pale, her body slender and firm, her bottom well defined. I gently kissed her neck and at the same time took one of her breasts in my hand. It was huge and I loved the way it felt. Her nipple reacted immediately, becoming as hard as a coffee bean. She slowly turned round and kissed me on the lips. Her legs parted slightly and her body sought mine.

*   *   *

It was about 7 am when we took a rest, both of us exhausted. My back was scratched all over, and she apologised to me but I just laughed. Sweat had literally soaked the bedsheets and she dried my forehead with a tissue. Apart from screams of pleasure and the usual sexual incitements, shouted in three different languages, we hadn't spoken to each other. We felt at ease but, nevertheless, I knew questions were on the way.

I expected a lot of silly questions, but she simply said:

'You can't fool a woman in bed. In bed you don't wear your designer clothes and you can't make up silly stories. I am not that stupid and I have made a living out of men since I was a teenager. You are wild and you are used to dominating people. You simply walk all over them. No kids' stuff here, Italian boy, but if you don't want to talk, I am not going to ask.'

Tenderly I bit one of her nipples and, looking straight in her eyes, I murmured: 'You are right of course, but it is too long a story and you need some sleep now. Enough

valerio viccei

to know that I am an alien from another planet.'

She smiled and, before exhaustion took over again, she managed to whisper: 'It wouldn't surprise me at all, baby.'

It was late afternoon before we sat around the small table opposite the fireplace. We had both had a good shower and a strong cup of coffee; it helped my battered body to recover some of its energy. She looked happy, almost a different person from the one I had talked to the previous night. I was almost tempted to undo the belt of her robe and make love to her again. My erection was evident and the small towel tied around my waist made a very inappropriate cover. She smiled and, as if to make her point clear, she added one more knot to her belt. I raised my arms in surrender. We both laughed. We had something to eat and very little was said. It was not that I was embarrassed, but I knew that she had seen through my lies and it would be stupid to continue with the bull of the previous night.

What was I going to do, could I trust this stranger and tell her who I was? I had genuinely good vibes about her, as well as needing someone to whom I could speak freely, someone with whom I could be myself. The wounds of recent betrayals had not healed yet — they never would — but I do love women and I didn't want past disappoint-ments to affect my future intimacy with them.

'Right, Susan, where do we start?'

'There is no need for this, if you don't want to.'

'Need it is not the right word. I deceived you with a lot of lies and I feel I owe you an explanation. You may not like what you will learn about me, that's all!'

She kept on spreading some butter on a slice of bread, slowly and almost mechanically. Her mind was clearly focused elsewhere and she had a funny smile on her face.

'It seems to me that we both lead double lives and that very unusual circumstances have blown our cover, Gigi. I also think this makes us very similar and ready to talk about our true selves: what do you say, "reporter"?'

'OK, Susan, if your own story will convince me that we are tuned on the same frequency, I will tell you mine, but don't forget that I will have to struggle for words. Is it a deal?'

'Here you go, "reporter", walking all over people again and dictating the rules, but I shall make things easier for you. Men have always expected that from me.'

Susan spoke slowly and for a long time. She laughed sometimes and tried to be detached from her own story, but I could detect a lot of pain and even some shame in her words. Her story was sad and I was moved even though I was accustomed to suffering, violence and exploitation. The girl had gone through a lot; she had reached the bottom but found her way back. She was a survivor and this was the bond that would bring us closer. I trusted her then and, to my great satisfaction, I have never regretted it.

What could I say to her? Words do not heal wounds and mine would be very ineffectual in any case. I am not going to give any detail away, as a matter of respect and loyalty towards her, but I want her to know that she remains one of the most trusted and caring companions I have ever had. I owe her a lot.

It was now my turn to open my heart and let the memories flow, to arouse the pain and repress my rage. My English was poor, but she was patient.

'Are you ready for this?'

'I can't wait,' she joked.

And so, I told her my story. I had been living a lie for months now and I wanted my past and my identity back. I didn't want to be Gigi anymore, I wanted to be my real self, Valerio Viccei.

'OK then. I am thirty-one and my real name is Valerio. I am Italian and I come from a beautiful town near the Adriatic coast. Its name is Ascoli Piceno and Rome is not too far away. My family have always lived there and so have all my ancestors for at least two centuries. Mom and Dad are both alive and are the loveliest parents I can think of. We are very close and I consider myself an extremely privileged son. They have been perfect in every way; it was me who screwed everything up. My dad is a retired lawyer and a man who has always considered the family his most valuable possession. He denied us nothing, and in return he only expected respect and good results at school from us. I have a brother and a sister, both younger than me.

'My mother is a beautiful and sweet lady who has worked hard to keep the family together and is still working nowadays. She owns a furriers shop which she inherited from my granny. I can't think of a better mother and I love her to death. I fucked up my life because it was my own choice. I have no excuses and my family are the ones who suffered undeservedly because of what I did. We are well-off and money has never been short. We children have not been spoiled, but were denied nothing: the best clothes, a bicycle at ten, motorbike at fourteen, car at eighteen, university at nineteen and so on. I studied law, but only for a brief spell. It was a total failure.

'I was clever at school and although I rarely spent time over my books I could easily stay abreast of my chums. Discipline and abiding by the rules were the real problems! At thirteen I started to show my true nature. I had a bad temper and was keen to fight everybody over the dumbest thing. I wouldn't take no for an answer and soon led my own little gang. I was picked up by the cops a few times, but the family's good reputation and my mother's tears had the better of them and I was spared the cells. I was a thorough little son of a bitch, no doubt about it.

'As soon as I was in my teens, my free time went on the three main interests that were later to bring me the greatest satisfaction, but also to be the biggest source of trouble: women, firearms and politics. In Italy, as elsewhere in Europe, the early 1970s were punctuated by violent and mainly hard-left student protests, from which my home town was not immune. I hated those scruffy and arrogant bastards. They were bullies and cowards, but they were numerous as well and they controlled all the schools and factories. Italy was like Paris and Paris looked like every capital of Eastern Europe: commies everywhere! A series of physical confrontations with

valerio viccei

those bastards characterised my high school years and I started to carry a gun on any occasion when the cowards outnumbered me and threatened me with severe violence. I was a target looking for targets and this did not escape police interest. They were soon after me, with the result that I was after them too. A vicious circle that spelt trouble!

'On 6 January 1972, a powerful explosive charge, planted next to the coaxial cables of a major national TV relay station a few kilometres from my home town, was detonated causing a total blackout on all domestic TV sets, and over a wide stretch of the Adriatic coast. A few days later I found myself behind bars. My parents faced the stigma of an arrest that was to upset the course of their lives and permanently scar my own. I had assembled and planted the charge because I hated the bloody socialist-controlled TV. I was seventeen years old.'

I kept talking for quite a while and Susan didn't interrupt me, she just listened and smiled from time to time. Although I felt relieved and I had no doubt that I was doing the right thing, I also had to struggle against my now over-developed caution. My life had been a real mess and most of my experiences would horrify even a hardened bandit. My past was scary and so were many of the outstanding charges against me. I realised that I couldn't afford to go any further, not at this stage of our relationship anyway. None the less, recalling my past, buried for so long in a dark corner of my memory, initiated a chain reaction, an unstoppable process that reopened fresh scars. I can see myself then as if in a photo

too fast to live

in an old family album. I am much younger, my glance is one of arrogance mixed with total boldness. Those were times when I used to learn Nietzsche by heart and burn down the offices of extreme left-wing parties. I admit that one of the best things written by this great philosopher inspired my life for many years.

'For believe me! — the secret of realising the greatest fruitfulness and the greatest enjoyment of existence is to live dangerously! Build your cities on the slopes of Vesuvius! Send your ships out into uncharted seas! Live in conflict with your equals and with yourselves! Be robbers and ravagers as long as you cannot be rulers and owners, you men of knowledge!'

I am today a more mature and much quieter individual, but the same fire of twenty years ago still burns within my being: my steely determination hasn't softened, the explosions of hatred and anger are equally as dangerous as they were then. I am equally as anti-Communist and uncompromising on certain political and social issues, with the sole difference that I have learned to control myself. I am more individualistic and no longer wish to change a world which seems to suit billions of people. I think of myself as a metropolitan predator and try to live as such. I have abandoned the rarefied, pure air of my idealised forest and travelled all the way down to the polluted town. I switched targets and instead of destabilising society I long to make money just like its most respected citizens do. Money is power to

valerio viccei

them, whilst it was just self-sufficiency and the prospect of a good life to me.

I am not violent, I am not filled with hatred and longing for revenge and there are no chips on my shoulder, but I can't abide by rules and values in which I have no faith. A predator doesn't ask, ever, he simply takes what he likes and can afford to grab. He doesn't feel remorse; he follows his instinct — that's his only rule!

Since those far-off days of 1972, when I blasted the TV relay station, an incredible sequence of happenings marked my existence, but one permanent thread remained unaltered: my attraction to women, firearms and all sorts of adventure. Something equally dangerous was slowly added to this already volatile mixture, my contempt for honest labour rewarded by a fixed income.

Like most youngsters with similar tendencies, I went through an apprenticeship of petty crime, joyriding and trouble-making. This was a very brief experience, not satisfying enough for a young man who gloried in his physical strength, lethal weapons and predatory instinct.

I obtained my grammar school leaving certificate a year early and was able to enrol in the law faculty of a university close to Ascoli. I was not, however, destined to follow in the footsteps of my father and so many of my relatives and forefathers. As time went on, one arrest followed another, most times over the illegal possession of guns. I always managed to get off without conviction and without much trouble either, given the absence of firm evidence against me and my shameless denial of any involvement. On the other hand, prison was to serve me

too fast to live

as a sort of training ground, where pacts were sealed and partnerships established, the place where I could build up useful contacts and a good reputation.

I was tough, strong and extremely quick with my fists, I took no shit from anybody and never pulled out of a fight. The local press focused on me and I was hated by the police more than anyone else in town. I deserved and could command respect which, of course, I managed to exploit to the full. In a country where organised crime was such a common thing, it was hard not to get involved with it, but I was able to keep out and always worked on an ad hoc basis, with partners drawn from a restricted circle of friends.

In over twenty years, I have never compromised on anything. I have always been my own man and chosen whichever accomplice or target I thought fit. I was the planner and the leader in the field as well; I always took the major risks and never tried to hide from the responsibilities that my rank implied. I was always the first to go in and the last to leave and that is the only way to command respect and loyalty.

As I have said, the first serious crime I ever committed was of a political nature and many others followed. In the very beginning I was just following my instinct and the instructions of more expert, better organised militants. Later I started training with determination and passion. The fact that I managed to get in with high level operators, mainly due to the various contacts made in jail, gave me the chance to be accepted by an active terrorist cell existing in Ascoli. This new experience, as well as fostering an already ardent love of weaponry and paramilitarism in general, further illustrates my natural tendency to pursue the most controversial aims, just as long as action and excitement are involved. The brief but active period spent in close contact with this group meant not just easy access to an endless source of firearms, forged documents and other practical stuff, but also quick mastery of operating techniques, which proved to be trump cards when transferred from the military to the criminal field!

My friendly relationship with Gianni Nardi, the leader of the cell, who was to be killed in a mysterious car crash while on the run in Spain, led me to meet an extraordinary little guy who is still regarded as the most dedicated and dangerous right-wing terrorist ever to declare 'war' on the constitutional powers. His name was Giancarlo Esposti and, like most of the people I was spending my days with at the time, he died violently, ambushed by a special SAS-style police unit and killed amid a hail of bullets. He was, together with other terrorists, rehearsing the final plan to assassinate the then Italian President in June 1974. The episode is still surrounded by mystery and only very recently has it come to light that the cell had been penetrated by the security services. The name of Gianni Nardi has also been found on the secret list of people belonging to the now famous 'Gladio' organisation which has been, and still is, the focus of major inquests promoted by the NATO allies. It was founded in the fifties with the aim of providing the civil population with the means of fighting

too fast to live

an ever-possible Communist takeover in Italy, and the fact that a much convicted terrorist could be a recruit of such a restricted number of people is highly suspicious.

Anyway, ten years later, my limited participation in the group and my involvement in some of the operations it carried out cost me a charge of attempted mass murder and membership of an organisation whose aim was to subvert the institutional powers of the State. I was tried in absentia on the strength of deceitful depositions made by my ex-wife, and acquitted of all charges while already in custody in the maximum security unit of Brixton prison.

I was briefly interviewed by the authorities in a makeshift prison box-room normally used for strip-searching inmates coming back from visits and in the absence of a lay jury. This was a farcical and unconstitutional proceeding, nevertheless there was a lot of pressure from the secret services and other obscure forces who stood to gain from my conviction.

It should be mentioned that, in common with other present and former members of hardline right-wing paramilitary organisations, I had previously suspected certain elements of the secret services, Carabinieri and some of their private informers of penetrating our organisation and perpetrating cut-throat policies in order to throw the country into chaos and justify an army takeover. A number of convictions handed down over recent years have not only served to confirm these hypotheses, but have also landed many members of these State organisations in jail. Securing my conviction in this particular case would have eliminated a most inconvenient witness and even if I was acquitted, my credibility would have been permanently damaged.

With the death of my friends I found myself completely cut off for several reasons, but mainly because the few who survived had been arrested and many others had been forced into hiding. Huge amounts of weapons and explosives had also been discovered, leaving the police and the investigating magistrates with the feeling that the whole organisation had to be fully destroyed there and then. By now my training, my potential and my detailed knowledge of daring operating techniques had reached their peak and this could only lead to one thing.

It was during the summer of 1974 that I pulled off my first armed robbery. I was only nineteen years old and this was just the start of a spectacular life of crime, and the waging of an all-out war against me by the police force of my own and other local towns. Due to lack of hard proof and my own ability to derive full advantage from legal technicalities, my prison spells remained very brief until November 1975 when, as usual, I was arrested on the strength of an informer's evidence and charged with using a firearm licence, made out in a friend's name, in order to buy high calibre guns from a number of suppliers in Rome. I denied all knowledge of this, but the police had resolved not to let me off and, by blackmailing various shady characters gravitating around my circle of friends, they obtained false statements against me.

Because of this, I had to spend six months on remand,

too fast to live

the maximum permitted for this type of charge. As it later turned out, these six months were to be crucial to my future!

By now I was twenty. Being completely free of school and with almost unlimited financial resources, I was dedicating most of my time to what nowadays would be too risky a pastime — chasing girls. Typical of the average Italian male, I had a steady girlfriend and, at the same time, several others all living in the same town and all aware of what I was up to!

I was restless and always on the lookout for new experiences and exciting adventures. During the summer leading to my latest arrest, although still 'engaged' to a very pretty girl by the name of Patrizia, to whom I often behaved disgracefully, I met a very attractive and wealthy girl named Noemi. This was no chance meeting, as, like most of the Ascoli middle classes, I was spending the summer at San Benedetto del Tronto, a well-known tourist resort on the Adriatic riviera. Noemi was on holiday with her parents, staying at the best hotel, wearing the most expensive clothes and attracting the glances of most of the male population. She was good looking and very flash, more than enough to attract a predator like me. We were introduced by a mutual friend, an ever-giggling young girl, the daughter of a local Senator. Membership of the same social group is important in Italian middle and upper class provincial circles. Besides, Noemi had not yet heard of me as she came from the far-off Viterbo countryside, beyond the range of the increasing publicity my repeated arrests had by now attracted.

We both sported the same designer clothes, wore expensive Rolex wrist watches and spoke faultless Italian. We moved in the same circle of friends and were clearly attractive individuals by any standards, and, as a result of this, everyone in the crowded disco seemed to be aware of what was about to happen. All eyes were turned on us, among them those of my girlfriend.

The next day I turned up outside Noemi's posh hotel on my new showy Kawasaki maximoto and a few minutes later off we went to a deserted stretch of fine sand, kissed by the Mediterranean sea.

The relationship I had with my home town was one of love and hate and although everybody knew of me and my repeated 'brushes' with the law, my personality, good breeding and frank smile helped me to get away with almost everything. To the extreme discomfort of the local police, I was universally accepted and, owing to a very peculiar set of values, my behaviour was not even seen as anti-social. It was for the same reasons, I suppose, that Noemi's parents could not help being favourably impressed by my manners and education.

The holidays were soon over for Noemi and her family, but what was to have been simply a midsummer flirtation between two complete strangers soon developed into something more serious and every weekend I started to call for her in my new BMW. At first I used to stay in a local hotel, spending my time in the company of Noemi and her parents who seemed, by now, to have accepted what amounted to a proper engagement. After a

too fast to live

few weeks, at Noemi's request, I began to stay in a villa belonging to her grandmother, who had outlived her husband and was living on her own. Very soon I became a great favourite of hers and was treated as one of the family.

Ignoring the risks that complete sincerity always implies, I told Noemi about my double life, withholding no details whatsoever of my illegal activities. She, a well-bred young lady from a wealthy family, responded with passive acceptance mixed with curiosity. Besides, she had already fallen in love and mystery, action and a thrilling sense of the forbidden must have made me all the more fascinating in her eyes.

As already mentioned, November brought with it my arrest on a charge of illegal possession of firearms just a few hours before Noemi, taking advantage of her parents going away for a short break, arrived in Ascoli on a totally unexpected visit. As soon as she learned of this, she realised that the main problem consisted of keeping my arrest secret from her folks. This turned out to be impossible and when my past life emerged for what it really was, Noemi was forbidden all contact with me, even by letter. By now, however, the polite and well-educated young girl had picked up some of my characteristics and, after a fierce struggle with her mother, she proved this point beyond any doubt. Although threatened with disinheritance by her parents, she left her home town for Ascoli.

The passage of time, occasional prison visits and plenty of letter-writing soon forged an even stronger link between the two of us. I was only twenty-one and completely unprepared for marriage, let alone any other ties or commitments. My life was still based on total independence from everyone in every way, while my permanent feeling of unfulfilment embroiled me in a perpetual chain of competitions with myself and others, often over the same female. I could not change.

Once out of jail, however, I had to make a decision whether to adopt some degree of responsibility, since Noemi had given up everything just to be near me and was, in fact, living with my parents at the time.

It was as proof of my respect and gratitude towards someone who had devoted her life to me without hesitation, as well as the affection she showed me, that convinced me this was the woman who deserved the highest reward that love could earn — and so it was that we became man and wife on 26 June 1976.

The two sides of the family were reconciled to celebrate the occasion. Everyone cherished the hope that, as a young husband, I would now alter my way of life and opt for a normal existence, especially in view of the huge fortune belonging to my newly acquired parents-in-law who, moreover, had no male offspring and stated their willingness to provide us with responsible positions at home or abroad. Needless to say, we both declined the offer!

Despite a life of permanent tension and constant evasion of the police, who were always in hot pursuit, we were happy and quite devoted to one another. After all, we were two young people from excellent family backgrounds, both healthy and clever. We seemed to have everything going for us and my problems with the law appeared not to bother anyone. There was certainly no shortage of money, as I had now begun to 'work' on one job after another. It seemed that hardly a week went by without some local bank being raided. The police knew only too well who was behind it all, but they never had a scrap of evidence which they could use against me. The fact that we surrounded ourselves with every luxury — the most expensive cars, jewellery, clothes, first class restaurants and hotels — made us all the more tantalising a target for the local Special Branch, who were lying in wait for that one fateful slip. As in every worthwhile story, the slip inevitably occurred.

An accomplice of mine, who had been working with me for a while, decided that he had become clever enough to organise a job himself and pull it off with other people. What was worse, he was going to hit a place under the jurisdiction of my home town cops!

I was spending most of my time in Rome and only went back to Ascoli once a fortnight to see my parents and to plan one of the robberies that I would carry out in the coming months. I knew nothing of this guy's intentions, if I had, there would have been big trouble. There are rules in the underworld which cannot be broken without facing serious consequences and he was about to do something extremely disloyal to a 'senior' partner — working with other people and in his own hunting territory!

One night I received an alarming phone call from my

mother who said that a bank robbery had been carried out near Ascoli and the cops had been round as usual. I asked about the technique and details, only to find out that it was a carbon-copy of my previous robberies. I smelled a rat immediately and a couple of calls led me straightaway to the lad whose name was Roberto Ciccanti. Having a solid alibi, I decided that I could take the risk of going back to Ascoli even though the local police would be furious. I needed to see Ciccanti before he was caught!

After a quick and highly charged meeting with him, I realised that he was about to be arrested and told him so, advising him to leave the town and go into hiding. He dismissed my suggestion and was lifted by the police the next day. One of his new accomplices had grassed him up and also mentioned my name with regard to other robberies which I had committed. Ciccanti and his new partners were offered a deal by the prosecution and they immediately agreed to give evidence against me and my friend Guido. By the time this took place I was in Rome again and already looking for a safe house. I managed to avoid arrest for over five months but during this period I was tried in my absence and sentenced to eight years. I was finally arrested after a shoot-out at Genova Central Station and had to face many more charges regarding other robberies, illegal possession of firearms and minor crimes.

Things looked pretty bad and the prospect of spending a decade in prison was a conservative estimate. I started to work hard on my case and tried every trick in the trade in order to get out of prison. I fought against my lawyers' advice and Guido's pessimism, but in the end we were both let out on technical bail. Only 30 months had passed and I was free once again. My familiarity with defence tactics had borne fruit, but the police were not prepared to let me get away with it so easily. Although out of prison, I remained under police surveillance. I was not only forbidden to leave my own district, but had to report twice daily to the local police station. I knew only too well that my freedom hung in the balance and that, even if I managed to avoid making any slips and continued to keep to the letter of the conditions fixed at the time of my release, the final judgement was still due on the robbery offence, making my re-arrest inevitable.

I tried hard to keep away from trouble, but I also had to make sure that Ciccanti and his little gang of rattlesnakes were going to change their version when the appeal was heard. Guido and I made them an offer they could not refuse and, in exchange for their own safety, inside and outside prison, they agreed to alter the substance of their testimonies. The appeal was heard while I was again behind bars for having allegedly breached the bail conditions, but things had been carefully organised and, faced with the new evidence, the judges had to clear me and Guido.

All of this happened in 1981 and I knew that from then on my life could never be the same again. Arrests, convictions and acquittals became so frequent that I can't honestly remember how many times I went through the prison gates. Everybody knew I was guilty on all occasions, but lack of firm evidence or my own subtle manipulation of legal technicalities always saved my skin!

There is nothing honourable in saying that I was considered by the authorities and the police as public enemy No. 1, but the fact that in all the robberies committed there was hardly a trace of violence helped to create one of those myths which usually manage to drive the establishment insane.

It was a cold morning in February 1983 when I finally ran out of luck. What happened was something that I can only compare to a real nightmare.

In the very beginning things did not look too bad, not much worse than they had many times in the past anyway, and the fact that I was arrested for a bank robbery committed a few miles from my home town wasn't too big a deal. There was no evidence against me, Antonio or a third chap called Sergio 'Piglet' Di Mattia. Unfortunately, whenever a robbery took place within a radius of a hundred miles, I was the prime suspect and the cops never failed to turn up and carefully search my premises and those of my closest friends. By the time the police obtained a search warrant from the local prosecutor, Antonio, Sergio and I had split the money and stashed it away, together with the most compromising equipment.

At this point I must explain something to the foreign reader. All Italian banks used to have what they called a 'bait bundle', a wad of bank notes that was always kept in the bank's safe and never touched by the staff. All the money, usually used notes and made up of medium

too fast to live

denomination bills, was photographed by the Bank of Italy before being issued to the bank, and the film — together with a written record of the serial numbers — was retained by the Central Bank so that it could be checked any time it was needed.

The reason behind this apparently pointless exercise was rather subtle. Robbers usually base their technique upon the surprise and time factor, quickly grabbing all the cash they can lay their hands on and leaving the premises as fast as possible. Usually there is no time to check what you get out of the safe, which is something left to a later stage, but where the 'bait bundle' was concerned it would all be pointless anyway. It was real and used money, the serial numbers were not consecutive, therefore there was no visible difference. Inevitably, robbers took it and if the police were lucky enough to find any of the filmed notes in their possession the game was up for them.

Lacking further evidence connecting them to the robbery, the minimum charge would be handling and receiving stolen goods but, in the absence of a reliable alibi, you could consider yourself convicted.

Over the years and with a bent cop working for me, I spent quite some time trying to discover a way of identifying those damned bundles of money. Actually there was no firm rule but, in order to prevent very embarrassing incidents, bank employees did have to make sure they did not put that specific money in circulation by mistake. At the same time, it must not be too hidden from view or nobody would steal it. The trick, without going into boring details, was to be found in the colour of the elastic bands around the wad itself. Once I discovered this and I had had repeated confirmation that I was right, the first thing I did after a job was to get out the 'bait bundle' and stash it away. I would spend it much later, while shopping in Rome, or use it in post offices to send money to my friends in prison.

This time I did exactly the same thing but, as Sergio had not physically participated in the robbery, Antonio and I decided to give him half of the bundle so that he could get rid of it shopping around. We obviously warned him about its nature and he suggested that in a matter of hours the money, just over a few hundred pounds, would disappear. I then stashed away the remaining 'marked' notes together with the two guns we used for the job.

To celebrate our success, Antonio decided to buy some cocaine and, to that end, he asked me to give him some money for my own share, which I did. The following evening we all met in Sergio's house to check and weigh the stuff, with the result that the idiot had to pay us for his own share and Antonio and I were given back what we had paid to the supplier on his behalf. We had a nice evening and that was it!

Early next morning, the door bell of my flat rang with that typical insistent manner that one can only associate with police arrogance. The door was armoured and the locks so strong that surprise on their part was impossible. They had to be patient, as usual, and wait for me and Noemi to get up. In my flat I had a marvellous

too fast to live

hiding place, which I had specially built underneath a wooden cabinet. Once I was out of bed I checked that everything was in there. Among other things there was all my share from the robbery, a submachine gun, two hand-grenades, a silenced carbine and plenty of ammunition. Before I shut the door, and only as a matter of precaution, I took my wallet from the night stand and gave to my wife all the small denomination notes, keeping only what in Britain would correspond to twenties and fifties. I told her to put them in the 'hole', just in case, and I went to fetch a robe. Just a few right moves and everything looked perfectly normal: to find the hiding place they would have to demolish the house.

The police kept ringing the bell, but I took my time and walked slowly towards the door. When I looked through the spy hole, I immediately realised that some of them were not from Ascoli, but from the town where we pulled off the job. This was fine with me and I let them in.

By now, Noemi too had put on a robe and was making coffee for everybody. Having our place searched was so normal that we took things easy and tried to get it done without too much hassle. Besides, five or six armed policemen in one room don't make you feel too comfortable.

I was quickly shown the search warrant and told the reason for such an early visit. As I had rightly guessed, it was about the robbery we had pulled off two days earlier. They started searching the bedroom, quickly and efficiently, leaving most of the stuff unmoved. When they found my wallet, they asked permission to take the money and check it against a list they had with them. 'Ha,' I thought, 'the bait bundle!'

As expected, none of the large denomination notes were recorded and I couldn't suppress a grin of satisfaction. They seemed to be very disappointed and were about to go when one of the local cops picked up Noemi's handbag and asked her to take the cash out of it. As soon as I looked into her wallet my heart stopped beating: the notes she was supposed to have put in the 'hole' were there. Well, this was nothing too tragic as I knew that half of the 'marked' ones had been spent by Sergio 'Piglet' and the other half was in another hiding place at my parents' house.

The notes, about twenty-five of them, were on the table next to the list which one of the cops was checking; he suddenly looked up and smiled broadly. I knew immediately that something very wrong had happened!

About ten of the notes checked out against the list and I was asked whose money it was. Although it had been found in Noemi's handbag I naturally stated that I had given her the money the previous evening after I took it from our motorbike shop's till. I was immediately arrested on suspicion of robbery and all I could do was to give her a glance of deep disappointment. The silly woman, not yet completely awake, had put the money in her handbag instead of in the hole. The trouble I was in was even more serious than I realised!

The police put me in a patrol car and, under huge escort, we reached the Carabinieri headquarters; needless

too fast to live

to say every single officer felt obliged to come and have a look at me. For the first time in over ten years of undeclared war, they had got me by the balls. It was a great day for the law.

I denied all knowledge of anything and stated that I had an alibi which it was my intention to produce at a later stage when my lawyer and the prosecutor were present. I also refused to be subjected to interrogation, which was my right, and asked to be taken to prison as soon as possible, which they did in a matter of hours.

While still in a police cell, I heard that Antonio, too, had been arrested and a cop couldn't help bragging to me that some 'marked' money had been found on him too. It couldn't be true! I began to believe that my unbeatable system to spot the tricky bundle had let me down. What a cock-up!

Later I heard that Sergio 'Piglet' too had also been arrested and this did not sound right! How was it possible that each of us had ended up with those notes in his possession at the same time?

I was told by another eager cop that Sergio was clean, but that a witness had identified him as one of the robbers! That was crazy, as he hadn't played any part in it and had met us ten miles away from the bank. It had to be a fit-up.

We were shortly moved to a little prison near Ascoli and, once the interview with the prosecutor had taken place, we were allowed to leave the segregation block and were free to share the same cell.

I knew that I would be shipped out very soon, for

security reasons, so I tried to make the best of the time I could spend with my partners. In a matter of seconds we all realised what had happened, and Antonio and I almost wanted to kill Sergio.

The fat bastard, probably excited at the prospect of sharing the cocaine Antonio had bought, had repaid us with the money we had given him the day before. He simply got mixed up with the bank notes and gave us back the marked ones. As for his 'witness', it was a fit-up all right, but at that moment there was nothing we could do. I was moved to a maximum security prison five days later.

The weeks passed slowly and I was increasingly concerned over my alibi. The son of a bitch who had sworn to back me up all the way started to waver and I knew that the cops would break him sooner or later. There were no other elements against me, however, and as soon as the investigating magistrate took charge of the case, it seemed I was going to be committed simply for handling. Five years was the minimum I would get but I couldn't settle for that!

In a matter of weeks I was literally overwhelmed by trouble. Warrants and charges hit me from every direction and almost every town of the region. Someone somewhere had turned supergrass and scores of people were arrested. Guido and many other friends were behind bars: the source was reliable and causing unbelievable damage. I was being prosecuted for over fifteen bank robberies, arms trafficking, criminal association and so on. I was too shocked to take in the gravity of it all.

too fast to live

Noemi was always there, apparently as loyal and staunch as ever, not missing a single visit and writing long letters every day. She was feeling guilty about having given the police the opportunity to recover the bank notes, but that was irrelevant now and I avoided talking about it altogether.

Every time I was charged with a new offence, the screws came to my cell and put me back in the block because I had to be kept incommunicado until I was seen by the prosecutor. It was all driving me crazy, but there was nothing I could do about it except try to keep my sanity.

It was during one of these dreadful days, while I was totally cut off from the outside world, that a bloke in charge of distributing food and tobacco to the inmates managed to slip a newspaper clipping under my cell door. Had they caught him, he would have spent a month in the cell next door. A quick glance at his expression told me everything. I immediately knew that my problems had only just started.

A front page article said that weapons, cash and forged documents had been found in my parents' house! A feeling of fear and total defeat engulfed me for the first time in almost fifteen years. I was finished and my folks could well be in serious trouble because of me.

Even before I was charged with the various offences, I asked to be seen by the local prosecutor: a fair and worthy opponent who had never messed me about. He told me that the game was up and I should confess to avoid the suspicion hanging over my family. He 'knew' that everything belonged to me, but the fact that it had been recovered in my parents' house was something that could not be ignored. Some sort of deal was struck and I admitted to the charges brought against me. None of my family members were even questioned and the matter was dealt with by the courts in less than forty days. A three-year sentence was the outcome and this was only for guns and the ammo. I tried in vain to find out how on earth they had found the hiding place. It had avoided detection for years and only five people knew about it! Obviously, the fifty 'marked' notes had also been recovered and at this point even my attempt to beat the robbery charge seemed doomed to failure.

To top it all, one day Noemi stormed into the visiting room 'armed' with some bundles of legal papers. Her attitude took me by surprise as never, in almost ten years, had she ever dared to act so aggressively in my presence.

I soon learned that some cop had provided her with the transcripts of all my telephone calls and, with it, firm and unchallengeable proof of my repeated cheating on her, plus the names of mistresses, girlfriends and so on. I admitted to nothing and, as usual, maintained that it was all a set-up. Unfortunately, this did not work as she had already visited some of the ladies involved and had obtained full confessions. I definitely did not need this, not at all!

Eventually agreement was reached between me and Noemi that we would not argue any more about the past and that things would be sorted out once I was free again. The only other alternative was an immediate

too fast to live

divorce and her departure from Ascoli for good. She refused, saying that her duty was to be near me for as long as I needed assistance and care! I should have known better!

Despite such endless catastrophes, I couldn't let myself become overwhelmed by the tide of disaster which, if verified, could have kept me behind bars for the rest of my days. My restless brain went into action, fully supported by the loyal Guido, Antonio, Sergio, Rolando and, as usual, Noemi. The magistrates were taking no chances this time and, well aware of my ability to manipulate legal technicalities, they began to separate me from my co-defendants and to keep me on the move from one awful prison to another so that Sardinia, Sicily and other remote parts of Italy soon became a Mecca of pilgrimage for my wife and my mother, who continued to follow my trial with devotion.

I finally had to accept that at least one major trial was going to be held in spite of all our resistance. As expected the trial had some very tense moments. The supergrass himself was present, under strict protection and away from the cage where the fifteen of us were kept. Expulsions of some of us from the court room were marked by violent clashes with the police escort. Security, to an extent hitherto unseen in the town, surrounded the court building and armoured vehicles became a common sight around the court. In this atmosphere and with no proof other than evidence given by the supergrass, all the defendants were found guilty of all charges. I was sentenced to eleven, Guido and

Antonio to eight, and Rolando to thirteen years of imprisonment.

This latest conviction meant that I had now incurred a concurrent sentence of fifteen years. Another trial for carrying out the robbery for which I was originally arrested — plus another five — was due to be held very shortly at the Court of Fermo.

Things were looking very bleak and I needed a break to reflect very carefully on what I was going to do next. After consulting with my co-defendants and close friends, I reached the conclusion that a change of tactics was imperative since the same supergrass would again be the source of evidence and I knew that a further conviction was inevitable.

Although I had denied any involvement for over eighteen months, as soon as the next trial started I sought permission from the presiding judge to make a statement in which, to the amazement of one and all — defence counsel included — I pleaded guilty to all charges except for one. I refused to provide the names of those who had collaborated with me during the various raids but, as had been agreed, I anticipated that each one of them would assume his own responsibilities before the court. Of course, I did admit to being the mastermind of all operations and to having physically played a major role. I also made sure to exonerate Guido and another defendant — these two being far less implicated by the witness and, consequently, having a better chance of being acquitted.

We all benefited from this change of attitude and the

too fast to live

presiding judge himself had to agree that such a development meant he could allow extenuating circumstances to apply to all concerned, something that would not otherwise have been the case. This was exactly what I had been after!

The claim of extenuating circumstances having been accepted, the Court of Appeal was now obliged by law to hold a hearing within a very short space of time or face the release of all defendants. Again, nothing was left to chance.

After the hearing had been completed, resulting in another eight-year prison sentence, four of my co-defendants, belonging to the team led by my friend Rolando, got away in one of the most sensational escapes in Italian history, together with two other prisoners. The four, armed with a handgun and knives, forced their way past a number of prison officers and made their getaway. An officer was shot and others were seriously stabbed. The most senior prison officer himself received injuries which kept him hovering between life and death for several days. Weeks later the police managed to find the den where four of the wanted men had taken refuge. In the ensuing shoot-out, one of my friends was killed, two were seriously wounded and one finally committed suicide by shooting himself in the mouth. To be honest, it was a planned execution and the men were never offered a chance to give themselves up.

As a direct consequence of this, my friend Rolando and I, who were not even in the same prison at the time of the event, were kept under much closer surveillance and even higher security prisons were found for us.

I was living a nightmare and the pressure was slowly, but inexorably, becoming unbearable. There were not too many alternatives left to me, but I managed to hold out even under these circumstances and scored another tactical success. With the aim of deferring a number of appeal hearings and the carrying out of relevant prosecution enquiries, I finally adopted a stance which I would describe as self-accusatory. In other words, I enabled the police to locate and recover an impressive number of deadly weapons still in my possession and buried all over Ascoli. I also admitted to innumerable bank robberies, including raids for which I had actually already been acquitted and many others for which I was not even prosecuted.

This seemingly suicidal tactic did a great deal for both myself and my co-defendants, in that barely three years had elapsed since our arrest when we were all released. Having been arrested early in 1983, in fact, Guido and most of my other friends were freed in the summer of 1985, having spent the maximum permissible term in custody pending appeal.

I had to wait a few more months because of a technicality but, although having actually accumulated sentences of about thirty years' imprisonment, to the amazement of judges, magistrates and relatives alike, not forgetting the media, public opinion and Noemi, I again walked free.

Before my official release, I spent the few days left to me in prison imagining the various situations which

too fast to live

might await me outside. Although I had acknowledged my leading role in an unbelievable series of crimes, I knew only too well that the police and most of the investigating magistrates would never leave me in peace. My new attitude had been viewed with great scepticism, and those with long experience of me, of whom the then Chief Prosecutor at the Ancona Court of Appeal was one, had publicly stated that these tactics were only intended to achieve some obscure purpose. The old man was to be proved dead right. I had simply tried to exploit a loophole in the law and get away with the minimum sentence for the largest number of offences. The fact that things turned out to be better than I hoped for should not be blamed entirely on me!

As I walked through the main prison gate I knew that from now on my life would be spent in nerve-wracking anticipation of any single fatal slip. They would never leave me alone.

As though all of this was not enough, Noemi seemed to have changed recently. Her last two visits had been highly charged and although she did not say anything, I could detect panic in her body language and in her eyes! She had always behaved like an apparently devoted and faithful wife, never failing to turn up at the weekly prison visits nor omitting to write each day of the three long and hard years. I had a feeling that serious family problems might be brewing.

Following some perverse and typically female logic, Noemi had taken advantage of her complete freedom and independence to start various relationships with characters from the Ascoli underworld. These included heroin addicts, scum of the worst kind, parasites and muggers, people lacking education, good manners or even acceptable appearance. What is worse, they were all drawn from the very lowest social orders and belonged to a circle of people whom I had always treated with great contempt for the miserable way they lived their lives, people who were completely at odds with her former aspirations!

This incongruous behaviour obviously indicated a clear desire to belittle me and dissipate the reputation that my activity and battles with the law had inevitably created among the locals. The truth is, I should never have allowed her to stay in Ascoli once she discovered that I had been unfaithful to her. This newly acquired knowledge produced a complete change in Noemi and humiliated her so deeply that she felt entitled to deceive me. All of this could have continued indefinitely were it not for my unexpected release and the return to a status quo where I had access to the truth. What I discovered created real panic among those who had been so 'bold' as to console my wife while I was behind bars, but who had now gone into hiding. I found out everything within twenty-four hours of my release and the shock of such a sudden and painful humiliation, inflicted by someone whom I had held in the highest esteem, brought me great distress. I did not know what to do, but murder and then suicide seemed a fairly acceptable response to my betrayal!

Compromise has always gone against the grain with

too fast to live

me and the prospect of Noemi getting out of this situation lightly was not too appealing, but once again my sense of survival and desire to come out on top kept me calm and made me consider all the options. The solution which I finally adopted was largely due to my mother's tears and advice from my father, a sensible man who knew only too well where my temper and determination would inevitably lead.

So it was that I offered Noemi a means of escape: I would be ready to leave the country on condition that she left Ascoli for good, in order to save what remained of the family honour. The fact that Noemi had found the desire to destroy my image in revenge for my own infidelity never made me imagine for a second that she could also become a police informer and that she would conspire with them to have me captured and possibly even executed. Our relationship had lasted ten long years after all.

It was in this context that I decided to plan a robbery together with Antonio and thus rapidly obtain the money I was going to need while on the run abroad. Noemi's attempts to have me arrested and shot failed only because of lucky coincidences and my experience, but her commitment to the task was definitely total.

Over the following weeks Noemi kept the police informed of my movements so that all they had to do was wait; they would catch me breaking my bail conditions and I could be re-arrested.

So it was one afternoon when I set out with Antonio and Noemi to check out my next target. Noemi did her

valerio viccei

work well and I did not spot the unmarked police car that followed us.

We were on our way back. Everything had been quiet and I had had a good opportunity to check the jewellery shop without being noticed by anybody. We had also spent some time trying to find the safest getaway and this had proved a little more tricky. Thinking about it, I might need one more reconnaissance trip which was always a risk.

'Well, I see no problem in pulling this one off, old buddy. I would say that in a week's time we'll be ready. Finding the right spot for the car changeover may be the only tricky bit. What do you think?'

Antonio, as usual, didn't commit himself: he was always very quiet and greed was his only motivation.

Our trip back continued in total silence and even Noemi was quieter than usual. We were totally unaware that the cops had been following us for a long time and then lost our car as soon as we left the motorway, so we were relaxed and paying little attention to what was happening around us. Our blue Fiat approached the toll gate for Ascoli and it seemed to be free of vehicles waiting to pay the fee. This represented our last obstacle, the most dangerous and risky moment since our departure from the town a few hours earlier. If a road block or simply a police patrol were to stop us now, the direction we came from would prove our guilt beyond any doubt.

I told Antonio to slow down a little so that I could survey the toll station. I couldn't see anything unusual:

too fast to live

there were no other cars around, let alone police patrols but I didn't lower my guard for a second, as I knew too well that if the cops had laid a trap anything at all out of the ordinary would betray their presence. I kept scanning the area.

Less than a hundred yards separated us from the toll station. One final glance and I was almost convinced that everything was OK when something caught my attention. A radio aerial was projecting above the hedge bordering the station building. The car it belonged to was still hidden from sight, but by its size and colour it could only belong to an unmarked police car.

'Holy shit! There they are! Go straight ahead without stopping and round to the right. Forget the ticket!' I shouted to Antonio.

The car swerved with the sudden change of direction and raced off from the toll gate. At the same time two special branch cops emerged from behind the hedge, machine guns in hand. They made for the middle of the road, but Antonio was good at the wheel and he knew his job. Once again he showed that he had few equals when it came to running. The car dodged round the two cops, no trouble, and when I turned my head to check what they were doing, I spotted an Alfa Romeo collecting them, ready for the chase.

Antonio followed my instructions and, in the shelter of a bend, he turned into a dirt road making for a fast retreat. The silence in our car added to the tension, but there was not a lot to say: if we were caught outside the city limits, we were done for. All of a sudden, the radio scanner fitted to our car crackled into life. Code names and initials were being shouted into the microphones of the various patrol cars, reporting what had happened, as well as their positions, to headquarters.

The unmistakable howl of sirens could be heard against the throb of the screaming engines. A giant chase was on and from the number of cars deployed we could assume that we were in the middle of a very well-laid trap. Were it not for that aerial we would have been in the bag already! The police knew very well that if we could slip through their net and reach one of the minor roads of the hinterland, they had had it. That was our territory: nobody knew the area as well as we did. They wouldn't have a chance!

I had underestimated the extent of the police operation and how badly the inspector wanted me back in prison. None the less we made it. Two hours later, with lights out, our car slowly covered the last few hundred yards into Ascoli. Should the police stop us now, we would be committing no crime and arrest would be prevented, for the time being at least.

Antonio dropped us off and we walked quietly down to where our Golf was parked outside the main hospital. At this time of the night it stood out like a sore thumb, one of the few vehicles in the parking lot: the others belonged to the night staff. Tension had taken its toll and I was longing for a hot shower and a little nap . . .

'Stay where you are and don't make a move!'

'What the fuck . . .'

'Shut up and raise your hands above your head very

too fast to live

slowly, Mr Viccei. Right, now put them on top of the car roof and stay that way.'

A man had appeared from nowhere. He was clutching a Beretta M12 sub-machine gun, its breech pulled back and the brass of a 9mm shell, held by the tip of the magazine, shining under the artificial light of a street lamp. One flick of the trigger and I would be cut down there and then.

I recognised him immediately. Only a few hours ago he had been dancing around like a clown in the middle of the road, in a vain attempt to stop our car.

'Look, pal, why don't you put that thing down? Just remove the clip very carefully before someone gets seriously hurt!'

My words were dry and humourless, but I knew only too well that if he decided to play the tough guy, there was nothing I could do. I knew all the town cops from a long way back and they mostly played by the rules. Things were looking nasty.

A few other cops now came out of their hiding places and this gave me a little more confidence. For a second I had thought the man had cracked up and might do something silly.

'I'm sorry, Valerio, but you must come to headquarters. Instructions from above.'

The two hours spent at police headquarters nearly drove me insane. We all knew the score. It was obvious that they couldn't throw me in a cell there and then. Had the chase ended up differently, then the inspector would have had firm evidence that I'd violated the bail restrictions, we both knew that, but all he could do at the moment was to make a detailed report to the Court of Appeal and hope for an arrest warrant to be issued against me and Antonio.

I got into the car with Noemi. She drove while I sat and brooded over the whole thing as if I were watching a movie shot at very low speed. Many of the details I'd missed all along were now much clearer, the conclusion just one. It was a trap! I only wondered why they hadn't shot me straightaway. I said this out loud, without looking at Noemi. Noemi, for her part, was careful to say nothing and show no reaction. Her whole concentration was on driving the vehicle, but panic must have begun in her mind. She must have realised basic reasoning could bring me close to the truth, too dangerously close.

The next day dawned cold and grey, the sky was as heavy as lead, almost a mirror of my mood. I had slept very little and very badly, the few hours I managed to rest had not made up for the stress of the previous day. I sat on the floor of my brother's bedroom and checked the spring of a Walther PPK magazine. I had already decided that I would go armed to the Court House, so if there was any attempt to arrest me, the choice between life and death would be down to a mere flick of my right forefinger.

The gun gleamed under the light, its smooth lines and perfect finish illuminating my face for a second. My obsession with firearms was deeply rooted, they were my babies. I couldn't help thinking it was a great irony that one of my own guns seemed destined to be the

too fast to live

instrument of my death.

I gently pulled back the slide, inserted a shell into the chamber and settled the compact semi-automatic in a pocket of my bulky leather jacket. My life had been on the line too many times for me to be scared. I was just sad; I thought of my mother and father and the pain was almost unbearable.

* * *

Were it not for legal proceedings still to be investigated, I would not mind telling the reader what happened in detail during that morning of six years ago, but I must follow my lawyers' advice. The fact that at the time of writing I am about to be transferred to Italy in order to serve the remainder of my sentence and face further trials doesn't make things any easier. Telling too many details would simply imply further charges and a lot more trouble, not to mention terrible embarrassment to the police and the senior prosecutor. Enough to say that anything could have happened during that fateful day and I am glad that nobody got hurt despite my wife's careful planning.

It was about 1 pm when I left the Prosecutor's office. I was very close to him, while the Inspector trailed behind us. The corridors of the Court House were crammed with plain-clothes policemen, but they couldn't make a move without facing disaster and I was taking my chances. Noemi was sitting outside the same office I had just come from and must have told the Inspector that I

valerio viccei

was carrying a gun, but he had panicked and given himself away as soon as he walked into the room. I had no alternative left.

We reached the outside of the building very quickly. There were even more police and at least three patrol cars. I had to make the most important decision of my life and it was not an easy one. A bus was now slowly approaching the square opposite the imposing court building; tomorrow would be New Year's Eve and the streets were packed with commuters, the traffic was chaotic. I must keep calm!

Cynically, I saw the incoming bus only as twenty yards of metal and passengers between my back and the cops' guns. I literally flew over a ramp of stairs leading to the car park, ducking and diving between the vehicles, expecting the fireworks to start at any time. Luck seemed to be on my side for once, as some pedestrians happened to cross my path. There were only ten yards between me and the bus. Run, man, run!

I made it! I was almost run over by the blessed machine, but things were definitely looking better and my old training was automatically taking over. Several patrol cars set off with a screeching of tyres. The traffic came to a complete halt and one of the patrol cars went rushing in the opposite direction.

A short sprint and I was in the ancient part of the town, leaving everything behind me. There was no way back now. I was on my own. In a matter of minutes every single cop would be looking for me and I wouldn't be asked questions, not this time.

too fast to live

I knew the town like the back of my hand, so I knew where to go in search of help and safety, a place not too far away and yet outside the net that was slowly closing in on me. Darkness would be my saviour, but the sun was not due to set for a few hours, the longest I would ever live through.

The suspicion that Noemi had been shopping me all along the line had still not crossed my mind and this would give her the chance to try again. She had lost none of her tenacity and determination to get rid of me for good, but now she also had to face the horror of being found out. The false moves repeatedly made by the cops should have advised her that it was about time for her to lie and play her hand very carefully. I was a wounded animal at bay and an extremely dangerous one.

* * *

Less than twelve hours later I had slipped out of Italy – a wanted man but still free.

The journey had been comparatively calm and when the train entered Switzerland the border police hardly took the trouble to check my I.D. All the tension of the last twenty-four hours suddenly vanished. A lot of problems had to be dealt with, of course, and dreadful thoughts kept crowding into my mind, but I had burned all my bridges and was finally heading for France: my destination London.

I had to pass two more frontier checks before reaching Dover and the faithful Walther, now tucked into my waistband, represented a great risk. I should have got rid of it a long time ago and, in fact, I had been agonising over this decision since leaving Italy, only to conclude that I would feel totally lost without it. The time had come to make up my mind and we finally parted. The sense of loss was crippling.

When the train reached Paris it was late evening and the city seemed to have gone crazy. People were preparing to see the old year out and bring in the new one in just a few hours. I would celebrate in my own way, downing a few cans of undrinkable French beer and watching a TV programme in this horrible language.

Shaking my head and feeling the effect of the beer for the first time, I lifted the phone. I struggled with the instructions and the prefix for a little while, then dialled a long number.

'Mamma? Ciao ma', it is me . . . Yes I am fine and safe, don't you worry. Everything went as planned, but Noemi disappeared as soon as we reached Switzerland. Things start to make sense, I guess.'

My mother asked me questions to which I couldn't or did not wish to reply, but I could feel her despair; fear for my fate was already getting the better of her.

'Mamma, listen to me, I can't spend too long on the phone. You understand that, don't you? I will call you shortly, in a few days.'

Her sad voice, overcome with grief, felt like a blade piercing my soul. She asked me to make that a promise because she would live just for those brief moments. I swallowed the pain of hearing my mother's tears,

too fast to live

suffering as I had never done before. I put the phone down, the silence was unreal and then, all of a sudden, explosions resounded everywhere: it was midnight and the New Year had just started.

I felt like a drop of rain that had just parted from a cloud and was hurtling through the sky towards the unknown. I clenched my teeth and promised myself that I would never give up. I was determined to stay free and see my mother again. Despite everything I have done through all these years my folks have never wavered in their love for me and have always been loyal, staunch as only parents can be.

CHAPTER 3

Back on My Feet

Susan postponed her departure for a couple of weeks and our relationship was extremely satisfying for both of us. We had a lovely time and spent most of it in bed. Our trust was mutual and I realised that she was willing to help me in any way she could. She knew that once she left I would be on my own again, or back with the same useless people I had been with since my arrival in England.

She introduced me to some acquaintances whom she had not seen for a long time. These characters were a world apart from the sort of people I would have liked to meet, but circumstances were such that I could only appreciate her efforts to give me the chance to spend time with people to whom I could address delicate and very specific questions. I slowly began to understand many of the things that had been a mystery to me and were at odds with my continental experience of banks.

By the time Susan finally left for Stockholm I had become totally self-sufficient and confident. The 'cardboard' crooks I had recently met later introduced me to slightly less pitiful characters, with the result that I felt it was safe enough to ask them if and where I could get hold of a large calibre handgun.

After an endless number of risky appointments in the most unsavoury areas of London, I was finally offered a Beretta semi-automatic pistol: the deal seemed to be feasible because the lad who had discovered the middleman was also willing to raid a bank with me. So he said!

I was repeatedly driven to Hatton Garden and left to wait in a rented car for hours at a time, making me feel like an abandoned dog. I had to swallow my pride and resist the temptation to break a few legs, but despair was taking over and I felt I could not stand those low-lifers much longer. In the end, after handing out what seemed to me a fortune by Italian prices, I was given what looked like a toilet bag containing two different handguns and various ammo. As soon as I had a look at the merchandise I wanted to throw up! Considering my love for firearms and the quality of the weapons I had always handled in the past, the two 'objects' I now held in my hands looked like a joke. However, the biggest hurdle was over. I was now totally self-sufficient.

I spent the best part of the night cleaning the guns, only to discover that one was totally useless. It was a small revolver with parts missing and the wrong supply

too fast to live

of ammo! The next day I chucked this piece of junk in a dustbin next to the Hilton Hotel. As far as its barrel and firing mechanisms were concerned, the Beretta was brand new: the outside was, in complete contrast, badly damaged by rust. I was told that the gun had found its way to England from Israel soon after the Yom Kippur war, and had been buried since then.

Now that the main tool of my trade was finally in my pocket, I could spend long hours looking around London for a suitable target to hit. I promised myself that the first operation was going to be very easy. I did not know enough English yet even to order everybody down on the floor. Were it not for my British colleague, I would have had to rely on the international language of the gun!

My partner-to-be proved to be a real nuisance. He was a useless junkie who talked a lot and did not have a penny to buy himself lunch, but at least was prepared to do something in order to improve his circumstances. Unbelievably, he finally came up with a tip-off which, I discovered months later, he had obtained by double-crossing someone else. He told me of a private bank in the West End consisting of several floors but with no security and no video cameras. The office dealing with the public was on the first floor and manned only by two women: the money was also good. It sounded easy to me, but I was very sceptical and — against his advice — I went to have a close look at the premises.

The reader must realise that at that time my English was awful. Whenever I actually managed to put a

71

valerio viccei

sentence together, my pronunciation and accent still made it almost unintelligible. Well, what happened in that bank was the worst nightmare a bank robber on the run could ever have.

I suggested that we go inside together, smartly dressed, and speak very little. I would play the helpless foreigner who needed to exchange some money and would apologise profusely for having ended up in such an exclusive bank.

That was the original plan and it was working just fine, when my idiot friend started to ask questions regarding bank accounts, transfer of money and so on. The lady teller could not understand his English any better than she did mine and, very politely, picked up the phone and called a colleague from the offices above. I was very close to shooting my man there and then!

The guy who came down to see us was only trying to be helpful, but he started to ask all sorts of questions, including our names and nationality. I did not know what to say and had to let bozo call the shots, with the result that the bank employee must have thought we had just run away from Broadmoor top security hospital!

We managed to leave the bank without having to shoot our way out, and I did not know whether to laugh it off or pump a couple of bullets in my partner's ass! I decided to laugh.

This cock-up aside, I had to agree that the job looked extremely simple and, although I hadn't had the chance to take a proper look at the till's contents, the fact that the cashier had coughed up the change for my

too fast to live

foreign currency straightaway meant that the till was definitely in her office and so was the cash.

At this point the only thing I needed was transportation and I resolved to get it as soon as possible. I already had a Fiat Panda rented under a phoney name, but since the bank was situated just behind the Hilton Hotel and in the middle of Mayfair, I though a motorbike would be far more suitable. I asked my partner if he knew where we could steal a bike without too much trouble, but he didn't have a clue as usual and I had to find it myself.

Thinking about it, I chose the worst place in London but at least there was a great choice of bikes, as the parking lot was just opposite the headquarters of a well-known despatch riders firm.

Once I had identified the target, I went to a big store and bought a battery-operated drill; a heavy screwdriver and some bits and pieces that would be helpful in fixing the ignition lock. The bike was parked in Berkeley Square and my plan was to remove it by hand and take it to a little backstreet where I could work on its lock without rushing. Once this was done, my partner would follow me in the Panda. Should anything go wrong, we would meet in a cafe where he normally spent most of his time.

Things looked simple, or so I thought.

* * *

It was early afternoon and the traffic was still very heavy.

valerio viccei

I could afford to wait a little longer, but I also wanted to get on with it. I was carrying my gun, and working in the open made me feel hugely exposed. My partner had been living in London for many years and, although I did not trust him entirely, I had to rely on him for most things: this was still an alien country for me and I did not want to screw things up at such an early stage. In spite of my instincts, I had to follow his advice.

I told him to keep away from me and to watch the main entrance of the Pony Express firm. If anybody came running out of the building while I was still pushing the bike, he was to blow the whistle and I would know there was trouble. If everything went fine, he was simply to follow me to the back street and watch my back while I worked on the lock.

Everything seemed fine, nobody was paying any attention to me and when I got the Honda off its stand I did it very naturally.

In a matter of seconds the bike was leaning against the wall of a back street building and I was working on its lock with my tools. I tried to give the impression to the few pedestrians walking in the street that something was wrong with the lock and I was trying to fix it. My partner came up and said that when he left the square everything was still fine: nobody had seen anything. I only needed a couple of minutes to finish the job then I told him to jump in the Panda parked nearby and follow. I was not yet entirely relaxed because although I had ridden powerful maximotos all my life, I had never done so in England and traffic here goes the other way round!

too fast to live

A few hundred yards' ride and I was in Park Lane. As far as I was concerned everything was fine but, all of a sudden, I noticed a patrol car in front of me. This is a very common sight in central London and I tried not to worry too much; I simply overtook it and carried on. As I left the police car behind I heard its tyres screech and a siren began blaring. I couldn't help turning my head round, only to realise that they were after yours truly!

'What the Hell . . .?' I asked myself, shocked by the speed of events. Well, there was no time to satisfy my curiosity. All I could do was hit the throttle and try to put some distance between me and the police. This proved not too difficult because of the heavy traffic in Park Lane and in a matter of seconds I easily managed to lose them. I was about to relax a little when another police car tried to carve me up from the opposite direction! At the same time a third police car appeared from nowhere, its siren blaring. This was heavy; there was no coincidence here!

I seriously considered the possibility that I had just nicked Prince Charles's own motorbike! Had the situation not been so desperate, I would have laughed. Things were getting well out of hand and I soon found myself in the middle of a giant chase right in the heart of London. Only after a few crazy tricks, and repeatedly riding over the pavement, did I manage to get rid of the lot of them.

By the time I reached Buckingham Palace Road, there was no trace of police behind me; adrenalin was still pumping hard, but I was safe.

valerio viccei

I jumped off the bike and raced inside Victoria Station. My first experience with the London traffic had been a catastrophe and my lookout had better come up with a good explanation or there was going to be serious trouble.

I took the first train leaving the station and got off a few stops later, with the result that I was back in London in about half an hour. I slipped inside a phone box and dialled the number of the cafe where my partner was supposed to meet me. He answered the phone himself and sounded pleased to discover I was not calling from a police station.

'Listen to me, you asshole! You told me that everything was fine when I left with the bike.'

'Sure, Gigi, that's the way it was . . .'

'Well, how do you explain that in a matter of seconds I had every spare cop in the area after me, uh?'

'I dunno, mate, I was as shocked as you and I can't underst . . .'

'Shocked my ass. It was me on that bike not you!' I interrupted him.

He didn't reply straightaway and I could hear him talking to someone else. He came back on the line: 'Look it's embarrassing for me to admit this, but I think it could have something to do with the crash helmet . . .'

'What crash helmet?'

'I think you have to wear a helmet in this country!'

'You son of a bitch! You THINK I should wear one! Then why are you only saying so NOW, when you always told me you knew everything there was to know

too fast to live

about this nutty island? I'm gonna kill you, you bastard!'

I went on swearing and calling him names as long as I had coins in my pocket. Only a useless jerk would have let me ride a stolen bike along Park Lane without wearing a crash helmet. No wonder the police were so interested.

* * *

After the experience with the motorbike I should have called it a day or, at the very least, dumped my partner-to-be. Unfortunately, I was becoming short of money and I still needed someone who was more accustomed to English life than me. I had no real knowledge of the way things worked in this country: I did not know that the police were unarmed while on the beat, that armoured vans carrying cash were not escorted by armed security guards and so on. Nor did I have a clue how public transport worked, where police patrols were most likely to be found, what the most dangerous areas were, etc. Sure enough, I was learning quickly and the more fluent I became in English, the more I understood the habits and rules of British society, but in all honesty I did not feel I could pull off a job on my own yet. As a result, I decided to stick with the bozo and get on with whatever we had to do as best as I could.

There was still a problem concerning the bike. The one we had stolen in Berkeley Square had been found by the police and so another one had to be acquired. This time things went smoothly and I nicked a bike after I had bought two crash helmets. It was late evening and a long way from central London, so even my partner was relaxed and, in his own way, tried to be helpful.

Having repeatedly tested the bike in the area where we would work on the day of the planned raid, I regained some of my confidence. Also, the fact that for over ten years in Italy I had been used to confronting armed cops, armed security guards, armed customers and even armed passers-by, made this job look like kids' stuff. I was eager to go and, at the same time, keen to get rid of the nuisance I had to work with.

When the time came, as I had expected, my partner started to feel the pressure and, just ten minutes before we were supposed to reach the target, he started whingeing and moaning about the risks we were taking. When I could take this no more I told him that if he was so scared, it would be better for both of us if I had a go on my own. At least I would know where I stood and wouldn't need to watch out for his blunders.

He just mumbled something, had a leak for the umpteenth time in half an hour and finally nodded. I made one last check of our equipment and we left on the bike.

I was wearing a comfortable brown jacket, plain shirt and a woollen tie. The trousers' colour matched the jacket and on my feet I wore a pair of beige Clark's ankle boots with rubber soles. I had grown a beard on purpose and wore a pair of round tortoiseshell spectacles that made me look like a left-wing intellectual. I looked anything but suspicious.

too fast to live

As far as my partner was concerned, although I had tried hard to improve his appearance, he still looked like someone who had no business inside a private bank. To overcome this problem, I suggested that he could come in a few seconds after me when I was already very close to the cashier. Should she become alarmed by his presence, it would be too late as I would be in a position to prevent her from doing anything. I emphasised that a few seconds meant exactly that, because if he waited too long I would find myself in an awkward position: once the cashier had changed my money I would have to leave the bank. Bozo said that he understood everything and I should not worry. I did anyway!

I dropped him off just fifty yards from the bank entrance, which would give me time to park, get rid of the crash helmet and quickly scan the street. As agreed, he was carrying a dark nylon bag under his coat but no weapons; I had my Beretta tucked into my trouser belt and wore no gloves. They would look too suspicious and, besides, I wouldn't need to touch anything at all. Once I had secured the room it would be his job to get the money out of the till and fill the bag. He obviously had to wear gloves and, to that end, he had chosen an extremely thin pair of silk ones. He told me that this would improve his sensitivity! I said nothing, but cursed under my breath.

The front door of the bank looked like the main entrance of a nice private home: there was just a small brass plate bearing the name of the bank. The door was open and up a small flight of stairs there was a second door; this one was made of reinforced glass and its lock was controlled by a young girl acting as a receptionist. She was sitting a few yards away from it, inside what looked like a little control room. I knew that on my way out I would not need her co-operation as the lock could also be opened manually from the inside. She was no obstacle at all and wouldn't interfere with my work! I smiled at her through the glass and she released the lock straightaway.

'Good afternoon,' I said politely.

'Good afternoon to you too, Sir.'

I walked to the right, still smiling, but without saying any more. She did not pay the slightest attention to me.

I was now inside the bank itself. There were no customers and the two women I had seen during my reconnaissance visit were busy with their paperwork; they had not yet noticed me. Very good indeed! Instinctively I looked over my shoulder, hoping to see my partner arrive, but he was still nowhere to be seen.

The room was very large, one would associate it more with an insurance company than with a bank. There were just a few working desks, a few chairs, some pieces of nice furniture and nothing else: no partition glass, no cameras, no proper tills!

I was now standing opposite the lady working at what I knew to be the till and, as she noticed me for the first time, her expression was a bit puzzled.

'Good afternoon, Sir, what can I do for you?'

She had not recognised me and that was good; nor

too fast to live

had she shown suspicion of any sort. I could tell immediately that she was relaxed and efficient. Where was my man? 'I need to buy some foreign currency, US dollars. Would you mind telling me the rate, please?'

I sensed that she was about to ask me something, but I kept smiling and took a wad of bank notes out of my pocket: they were English fifties, held together by a gold money-clip. She seemed to change her mind and reached for a computer print-out of the various rates, which would give me some extra time. I took a further look at the room and saw that the other clerk was still facing the other way, concentrating on what looked like a computer screen; she seemed to be unaware of my presence. There was still no trace of my partner.

There was no time to spare. In a matter of seconds I would have to draw my gun or quit. While this thought was crossing my mind, my peripheral vision detected a shadow: it was him! I took a long breath.

My happiness vanished immediately as soon as I realised that the idiot was struggling with his silly gloves, clearly too small for his big hands: if the cashier lifted her eyes now she would scream her head off.

Without saying a word I went round the desk and quickly took out the gun, but the lady was concentrating so hard on what she was reading that she hardly noticed what was happening. When she looked up and noticed that I was standing so close, with a gun in my hand, she was overcome by shock! This was momentary, unfortunately. In the five following minutes she would behave like a women possessed!

valerio viccei

'This is a robbery. We don't want to hurt you. Be quiet and do not touch anything,' is all I said, and it cost me some effort because I had had to learn it by heart.

By now my old training had taken over and I tried to assess very quickly what sort of character she was, how she would react and how much trouble she was willing to give me. She sat still on her chair, apparently calm, then, all of a sudden, she grabbed the desk and pulled herself towards it, her right foot seemingly seeking something! I seized her by the shoulder to prevent her moving forwards, but at the same time she reached for the till and locked it, taking the little key in her hand.

She seemed about to put the key in her mouth and I had to struggle to get hold of her hand. I didn't want to hurt her. I took the key and passed it to my partner, telling him to get on with it. I replaced the gun in my waistband in order to deal with this lady as best I could. She really was a pain in the ass!

Having lost the key, the girl now began to scream her head off and, again, I tried to prevent her from doing so by acceptable means: I put my hand over her mouth and repeatedly told her to keep quiet.

I also had to keep an eye on the other girl who, unbelievably, still had her back to us.

My partner was making a real mess of the till. He had forgotten to unzip the bag properly, with the result that bundles of money fell repeatedly on to the floor. I closed my eyes and prayed that nobody would come in now: the lady was still kicking and trying to bite my

too fast to live

fingers, so I decided to lift her off the chair and make her lie on the floor. I tried hard not to lose my patience, but she really was pushing her luck. If I had to slap her, she wouldn't wake up until next week, but I have always been against this sort of thing so I let her struggle unharmed.

I told my man to be quick; I had had enough of this mess and the sooner we left the better. He said that one of the drawers was locked and there was no way to open it; we could go.

As I was about to get up off the floor, where I had been wrestling with my lady friend, a male employee came into the room. His eyes widened as if he had seen a ghost. He dropped some papers he was carrying and ran off yelling like there was no tomorrow. Time to go.

I let my partner go out first. I went to follow, but the lady did not seem to be finished with her performance yet and tried to get hold of my jacket. She was obviously brave and certainly crazy!

We reached the street in a matter of seconds and put on the crash helmets we had left on the bike. I got on it, turned the ignition key and nothing happened.

I tried a few more times to no avail, only to realise that my partner had already split and was running towards the Hilton Hotel like Speedy Gonzales. I also noticed that three or four male employees had just come out of the bank. They had not noticed me but were gesticulating towards my running partner. I drew my gun and gestured to them to back off. They scattered like a bunch of little mice!

valerio viccei

I now had no alternative but to run after my buddy who was about a hundred yards away. I took off the helmet and ran for my life. The cops would be well on their way to the bank. I caught up and told him to head for the Panda which, in case of trouble, I had parked in Curzon Street; two more minutes and we reached the car. There was no trace of the police yet and I thought we had made it, the mess up notwithstanding.

I had to shout at him a couple of times because by now my partner was very excited, thinking the area would soon be sealed off; he did not know that I had had my own route carefully planned a week before. In less than five minutes our little car was safely parked in a back street behind Claridge's Hotel. We had done it!

*   *   *

I now moved to a very smart area of North London called St John's Wood. I found a lovely little flat in the High Street and very soon got to know the local residents who apparently accepted me for what I said I was: a wealthy Italian reporter who was learning English and who travelled a lot on business connected with his family's financial activities. I had the time of my life and really enjoyed the fact that nobody knew who I was; I could act normally for the first time since I was a teenager and be appreciated by people for myself instead of for my reputation. I met plenty of beautiful ladies who were more than willing to spend time with me. I started to burn money the way I did before I left Italy,

too fast to live

on expensive cars, clothes, restaurants and hotels which I happily shared with my new friends. It was in this street that I met Helle, Peter, Pinkas, Eric and other characters who — one way or another — have played a big role in my life.

CHAPTER 4

Almost in the Bag

It was a cold January morning in 1987 and St John's Wood High Street wasn't too busy with people. I had just finished warming up the engine of my white Ferrari Mondial and exchanging the usual greetings with shopkeepers and neighbours, when my attention was drawn to an unmarked police car that kept patrolling the High Street. To be honest, I did not take much notice of it as the local police station was fifty yards from where I lived and from where my car was now parked. Nevertheless, my senses registered what was happening as odd; and in my line of business you quickly learn to trust your feelings if you want to grow old.

That afternoon I had an appointment with a stunning lady whom I had been stalking for months. I had finally managed to get a date with her and it was difficult to

valerio viccei

suppress my excitement and satisfaction.

My imagination was working on the possible outcome of this meeting. Careful planning would be needed in this delightful adult chess game. Openings and variations of openings were considered: her possible counter moves were not ignored and the whole business was giving me a sort of mental climax.

Unbeknown to me, the police had totally different plans for my afternoon, and very soon I would wake up from this daydream in a most traumatic way.

I moved away from the kerb very slowly and drove towards a carwash just a few hundred yards away. I hadn't even changed gear before I noticed a police patrol car on my left and another straight ahead. I woke up from my dream sharply, realising that they were there for me. I kept driving calmly, but activated the central locking, just in case. It was now my intention to leave the area very quickly and only a traffic light separated me from Wellington Road; I knew that if I could get there the police would have a hard job catching my Ferrari and an even harder one catching me. No chance! As soon as I approached the traffic lights, two patrol cars appeared from nowhere, sandwiching my vehicle from both ends.

A young, uniformed officer came straight to my door and pulled the handle, to no avail. He became jumpy and shouted at the top of his voice that I must open the door and hand him the car keys. Trying to keep calm and considering my options at the same time, I lowered the electric window an inch or so and politely asked him what was the matter. He did not buy this and kept yelling until joined by other colleagues.

I decided that the best thing was to play the wimp, hoping they wouldn't handcuff me there and then.

'Get the fuck out of the car!' was not too promising a start, but I began to gesticulate like a helpless foreigner caught in a situation bigger than himself. I got out. I was frisked, Miami Vice style, and, for good measure, the operation was then repeated twice more by different officers. They wanted to know how to open the boot and the bonnet in order to search the Ferrari, but no handcuffs had appeared.

I started complaining that I thought England was more democratic than Argentina and that such a show was totally pointless. Was there a senior officer to whom I could address my protest at being harassed and humiliated in the middle of the street where I lived?

One of the young policemen indicated a parked Metro with someone inside it. It was only ten yards away, but to me such a distance could be vital and I started scanning the scene. They politely opened the Metro door, I got in and nodded to the senior officer sitting at the wheel. I asked him what this was all about and if I could remove the Ferrari from the middle of the street. The man was clearly puzzled by my manners and stared at me. He did not reply to my questions but asked if the car belonged to me and if I could spell my name for him. I did as asked and again I stressed that it was my right to know what was going on and that, if I was not told, I would call my lawyer on the portable phone. Briefly, I was told that they had information — from a reliable source — stating that I was a wanted man in Italy and that I always carried a gun.

He spoke with the typical and forceful formality of a policeman who has spent too much time sitting at his desk. I pointed out that the reliability of this source couldn't be too good if the search had failed to produce any weapons. He said that if they had made a mistake I would be entitled to complain and that, to this end, I would shortly be given a brief written report of what had taken place. I kept on talking but I did not fail to spot one policeman looking at me through the car window and nodding nonstop. He was talking into his little radio and commenting on my features and clothes. Most of the other cops were busy with the traffic and still fiddling about with my Ferrari. I knew that I must act now. I started my ploy by telling the man sitting next to me that I had had enough of this farce and was going to call my lawyer. As I did so, I pulled the door handle gently, trying to be as natural as I could but then the man looking at me from the pavement came towards the Metro and, with a big smile on his face, said: 'Right, Sir, this is our man. An extradition squad team is coming to pick him up.' Then, to me he said, 'So you can stop moaning about your lawyer. I hope he's a good one as you are in deep shit, pal!'

The jerk was so happy that he paid no attention to my left foot until it kicked the car door straight in his face and he was lying on the pavement as though a truck had run him over. At the same time I punched the 'desk' man right on the nose, with the result that he was simply

too fast to live

too startled to react. Before the other police realised what had happened I was out and running like a man possessed. Luckily I was wearing my trainers and sports clothes, which gave me an advantage and I was already fifteen yards ahead of them when a little one literally jumped on my back. I got rid of him somehow and kept on running along the pavement, stopping only to hurl a big dustbin at my pursuers, with the result that they had to waste precious seconds in order to avoid it.

I soon found myself hounded by a pack of cops who chased me down a very narrow back street. I knew that if I did not put some distance between me and them, I would soon be cornered. I was just a few yards from the carwash and, although it was still early in the morning, many cars were already queuing up. Without hesitating at all I launched myself towards a small gap between the wall and the huge, spinning brushes! This carwash runs through a whole building; its exit is in Wellington Road and if I could manage to survive the 'wash' I would be able to put some distance between me and my pursuers. The police did not even try to follow me.

Drenched and as bruised as if I had jumped down Niagara Falls, I reached the other side of the road. My chest was heaving, but the sight of a policeman just a hundred yards away gave me new strength. I leapt over a low wall which turned out to have a drop on the other side of fifteen feet so that I was lucky not to break my ankles. On my left I noticed an open emergency exit door which I knew belonged to a building where a most exclusive clinic was housed. I went quickly inside and shut the door behind me, taking care to lock it with the metal safety-bar.

From the looks of the smartly dressed staff in the reception area I realised that my appearance must be pretty rough. I asked for the main exit, hoping to find a cab or a chauffeur at the wheel of a car; I had almost succeeded in my getaway and I was not going to stop at a possible hijack. Luck seemed to be on my side. There was an old guy standing by a shining Rolls. I pushed him out of the way and checked to see if the keys were in the ignition. They were not and I resumed my run, dashing inside Lord's cricket ground. They were doing some building work and the place was swarming with people in yellow helmets. I quickly took my blue cardigan off, put on one of the helmets and walked towards the opposite exit without rushing. Once out of the compound, I spotted a phone box just a few yards away. I decided to hide in there for a while and reorganise my thoughts, then couldn't believe my luck, when I saw a black cab coming slowly towards me. In a few seconds I was on my way to South Kensington trying hard to suppress my instinct to kiss the driver!

In just a few seconds I had lost my cover, my flat, my car and everything I had managed to gather in almost a year. I had nowhere to go, I could trust nobody until I made sense out of the police ambush and eliminated some suspects from the list of possible informants. I needed to find a familiar place where I could relax and think carefully about my next move.

All I had with me were a few hundred pounds, my

too fast to live

Rolex, a gold and diamond chain and the clothes I stood up in. Identity card, Filofax, portable telephone and all my keys were in the Ferrari and now the police had got them. If I did not act quickly they would shut down all my lifelines.

South Kensington tube station has a good taxi service and after I had made sure the one I was travelling in had left, I hailed the next available cab and asked the driver to take me to the Hilton Hotel. The Wolfe restaurant was just around the corner, so if they ever traced the cab driver, all he could say was that I paid the fare and walked inside the hotel. In fact, I left the Hilton lobby as soon as the taxi was out of sight.

It was a bit early, but Wolfe's was a place where I was well known as a regular customer. Nobody would take any notice of my appearance and the discreet washroom would give me the chance to improve on it and also lick my superficial wounds. More importantly, I would not feel observed. It is unbelievable how familiar faces and a friendly smile can give you back your confidence. Strangers always feed my paranoia!

I used the phone repeatedly and, in less than half an hour, I was joined by the wife of a friend of mine; her husband would find a message at home and would meet us later. Actually, of the two of them she had got more balls, and she was the one I was relying on to solve the most urgent of my problems. I had realised that as soon as the police sprung their trap and all hell broke loose, the nearby shopkeepers and their customers had all come out to have a better look at the show. Among them were the security staff of the Safe Deposit Centre where, just a few months earlier, I had rented a box.

The managing director and co-owner of the centre was a young Pakistani whom I had happened to meet a few times inside the premises and who was extremely polite. I was also on very friendly terms with all the staff and known to them as a wealthy Italian reporter who wrote articles for a certain sports publication owned by his family. What had happened that morning must have shocked them beyond belief!

As a general precaution I had always used to keep a spare safety box key and code-card in my friend Peter's flat and this now proved to be a winning move. In a matter of minutes Peter too had joined us at Wolfe's and I had to think carefully how I was going to get my stuff out of the safety box. My gun was there, so were my various passports, a lot of cash and my Swiss Bank Corporation documents.

I knew that St John's Wood was off limits to me now. More to the point, the Safe Deposit Centre staff had witnessed my arrest and subsequent escape. The million-dollar question was: 'Had they told the police that I had a box there?'

No matter what, I still had to make a move and I suggested that my friend's wife might go there as a new customer and rent a box herself. As the security guard in the control room did not know which box belonged to which customer, and his job consisted merely of making sure that personal codes were dialled correctly, she might then go back again in the afternoon with my card, my

too fast to live

code and my box key. Once she had inserted my card and dialled my PIN (Personal Identification Number) correctly, the security guard would have no reason to be suspicious as it was not unusual for a customer to have more than one box. Then, all she had to do was open the box with the proper key and empty it of its contents, consisting of a sealed nylon bag secured by a small but efficient padlock. In case of trouble the seal would prevent the police from accusing her of knowing the contents.

She left Wolfe's with her husband and I could only wait and see what would happen in the next few hours. If anything went wrong I would be in deep shit as that box was of paramount importance to my survival.

Things looked bad, but not as bad as they could get. My friends came back with worried expressions and without my precious nylon bag. The wife said: 'Well, Gigi, I did exactly what you said and everything was fine until I dialled your PIN! Nothing happened and the security guard, who had been smiling at me, started to stare. I kept trying but nothing happened and the computer failed to return the card. All of sudden this Pakistani fellow, the same one who signed my contract a few hours earlier, asked me if I could follow him to his office, which I did. He told me that I had just inserted a card which wasn't mine and dialled its correct PIN, which I wasn't entitled to do unless I had a specific power of attorney from the box holder. He asked me how I managed to get the card and the PIN. I simply replied that you were leaving the country in a

valerio viccei

hurry and had asked if I'd make the operation on your behalf. He told me that access to the box had been denied mainly because of what had happened earlier that morning, to which I showed surprise and shock. But he went on to say that, as the police had made enquiries, he had to protect himself and block the box waiting for further instructions. I was then politely invited to leave his office.'

The slippery son of a bitch!

I knew that the police could not possibly suspect I had a box there or they would have already had a search warrant or a court order, so I tried to figure out why the man was playing games with me.

In a furious temper I rang the Safe Deposit Centre in St John's Wood. I got hold of the manager, whose name was Parvez Latif, and told him that if I lost the contents of my box I would hold him and his family personally responsible for it and he could bet his ass it wouldn't be a matter settled by lawyers! He asked me to calm down and understand his position, to which I replied that I didn't give a fuck about him and his position: all I wanted was my stuff. Period.

My threats apparently hit the target and an agreement was reached. I was not too happy with it as the man sounded sneaky but I knew that time could only work against me. One of my relatives already had the power of attorney in my affairs and Latif was at pains to stress that if he turned up at the Centre, he would personally make sure that the operation was swift and discreet. He promised that the police wouldn't be notified. I did not

too fast to live

say a lot, I just pointed out that he was playing with his own life.

Just twenty-four hours later a relative came from Italy with another person. My relative limited himself to opening the box, the other man took the unopened bag and quickly left the premises. Latif had behaved well and kept his word. Now I knew that I could trust the man and I was not going to forget it.

* * *

At the time of this incident I was living with a Danish girl called Helle, who had moved in with me after leaving her job and her boyfriend of many years. I was not the kind of person who could commit himself as far as women were concerned, but Helle was a nice, understanding girl. I did not know how long it would last, but I decided to give it a try.

By lucky coincidence, she was in Denmark that day and this saved her from certain arrest and plenty of questioning. One of my first telephone calls was to Copenhagen. Once I got hold of her I made it clear that, under the circumstances, she was better off where she was. With the stubbornness that women often show at the most unsuitable times, she did not listen and after a few days was back in London. Her former boyfriend was still jealous and as soon as the news of my arrest and escape reached him, he made sure the police knew about her. When the police discovered that she was back, they tried to track her down to follow her. I managed to prevent this, not because I suspected she could be under surveillance, but because as a general precaution I forbade her to mix with old friends and acquaintances.

Unfortunately the police decided to check her credit card and one day I made the mistake of letting her rent a car. As soon as the bank received the company's voucher they notified the police and the GTI she had rented became as hot as burning coal. Luckily, however, something went wrong with its battery and we parked the car not far away from the flat we were then living in. Helle called the firm to notify them of the problem and their employee, following police instructions, asked her to bring back the keys so that they could replace the GTI. I told her not to bother with another car, but to return the keys and tell them where the GTI was parked.

Later in the evening we had an appointment at the place of a friend, close to Maida Vale. As I had something to do first, I told Helle that I would meet her there at 9 pm. Unbeknown to me, once she had left the car firm she was followed by a surveillance team and unwittingly led them straight to my friend's house. They waited outside, hoping that I would surface sooner or later. In fact I did arrive but my old training in Italy was now dictating the rules of my behaviour and I reached my friend's house by a very unusual route and on foot. I made my way into the building through a convenient block of flats. Should anybody be keeping the main entrance under surveillance they would not see me.

At about 3 am we decided to leave and a black cab was called. As soon as we got into the taxi I noticed an unmarked police car nearby. I felt quite confident; it was dark and I had a loaded gun with me; nobody was going to push me around. Helle did not notice the unmarked car. I gently told her not to worry, but that we were being followed and that serious trouble could break out at any time. Whatever happened, she was to stay put and raise her hands above her head. She started to shake but did not panic.

I wondered if the police had already called the taxi company and asked to which address the cab was directed; I could hear from the radio in the car that the operator had asked the driver to continue to his destination. The police followed us for a good five minutes. As our flat was next to Belsize Park tube station, the address we had given the taxi driver matched the place where the Golf GTI had been parked. We were not far away from Swiss Cottage when the crew of the unmarked car, obviously convinced that I had not spotted them and that we were therefore on the last few hundred yards of our trip, overtook the taxi. They intended to wait and pounce on me from out of nowhere. I immediately ordered the taxi driver to stop there and then. Although startled the man was smart enough to comply and drove off at lightning speed. My tone of voice had not been too kind.

I dragged Helle through a labyrinth of back streets until we reached a concealed entrance to the block where our flat was. The GTI was parked quite near, but there was no way we could be seen coming. We bypassed that street completely. I approached the door on my own with

valerio viccei

gun in hand, while Helle stayed behind. The coast was clear; nobody had tampered with the flat door. The various rigs I had left on it were untouched and that meant the police did not know where we were staying. As soon as we got into the flat I could hear many engines revving up; it was about 4 am. They had lost me again.

Paranoia was getting to me and I had to make a deadly decision; was I going out, gun in hand, to try to slip through the net that, in the morning, would certainly entrap me, or was I going to sit tight in the hope that they would not find the flat?

The protection the dark could offer me was too precious an ally to ignore; I would give it a try.

I climbed up the back of the house from a window close to the roof and, once I reached the top, I used a ladder as a bridge in order to reach a nearby house. I repeated this operation various times until I arrived on a large balcony. I could hear the tenants snoring in their bedroom. This house was opposite to where the noise of the police cars was coming from, but I still had to climb down and the only side protected from view was almost forty feet high. I got hold of a thick garden hose and, after tying it to a chimney, used it as a rope. I reached the ground safely but, to my disappointment, found myself in a blind gap between two buildings; I couldn't get out.

I decided to break into a ground floor apartment through a window and I hoped that my orientation was not totally fucked, as I could well end up where the police were waiting. I finally got the better of the window catch and, after crossing a room, I opened a

too fast to live

door and found myself on the staircase of an old house. I walked down towards the front door and through a glass panel at its top I could see the reflection of a passing patrol car. I put my ear against the wooden frame. Everything was quiet; no footsteps or whispers to be heard. I replaced the gun in my waistband, held my breath and in one single movement opened the door and hurled myself outside. I ran like a madman, without looking back, crossing gardens, and walking on garage roofs, jumping over fences until, finally, I knew I was safe again. I hid in a basement for fifteen minutes and then called a friend from a phone box in Primrose Gardens. I had made it, but I realised that London had become too hot for me, for the time being at least.

The extradition squad failed to trace the flat, but to go back was simply out of the question. Once again I had managed to escape, but it was hard to put together the various pieces of the jigsaw which would identify for me the source who was informing the police. The two episodes were definitely connected, but something was amiss as nobody knew about my most recent accommodation, apart from Helle and Peter and they were both beyond suspicion.

I did not know it, then, but the first police ambush was carried out following information received from the Italian anti-terrorist branch of Interpol, while the second operation was a present from Helle's former boyfriend. In other words, the first op had triggered the second and nobody had a watch on me or my movements. Obviously, I began to suspect everybody. Such interest

valerio viccei

from the English police was totally unjustified, unless my latest bank robbery had somehow given my identity away! It had not been a particularly clean job and although the media were instructed to keep quiet about it, I could not fail to realise that by robbing a branch of the prestigious Coutts Bank I could have drawn some unwanted attention.

I tried to recall the various details of the Coutts robbery described in Chapter 1 in order to establish a connection with the police ambush in St John's Wood, but the more I thought of it, the more convinced I was that the two things were not connected in any way. This period was extremely tense and I kept changing hotels and accommodation on a weekly basis. I was also seeing less of Helle, and was using more cocaine than ever before, which wasn't doing me any good. Before I had only used it socially and in very small amounts, just to feel at ease with people who were drunk or stoned, but now I did it with an entirely different philosophy and, being perpetually tense and in a sombre mood, it affected me badly. The old days in Italy started to crowd my mind again and I felt that something really bad could happen at any time. I decided I had to leave England for my own good, but I wanted to recover some of the money I had spent in the last few weeks and put a little aside for the ever-possible future rainy day, so I planned another job in Mayfair. It was to be an easy one, a small branch of the Midland Bank in Curzon Street, just a few yards away from the huge M15 building. All went well this time and I did not have any

Happy days: Helle and I in Denmark 1986.

Top: The black Ferrari Testarossa which I was driving at the time of my arrest.

Above: Some of my briefcase contents, its value over 1.5 million pounds.

Above: P.C. Steve Ashcroft displays cash, a handgun and other items recovered after arrests were made. (*Pictures courtesy of PA Pictures*).

Left: The Flick Diamond recovered by police in Belgium. Value: Four million pounds.

A girl in a million: Pamela Seamarks.
Above: Leaving Horseferry Road Magistrates' Court following my capture.

Top left: Pamela showing - off.
Above far right: Pamela photographed by Stephen Burton.
Below right: Pamela photographed by David Hooley,
News of the World.

A security camera captures me and my sidekick at work in Coutts Bank Cavendish Square, London. The raid came close to ending in disaster when I was trapped by hydraulic stainless steel panels behind the counter.

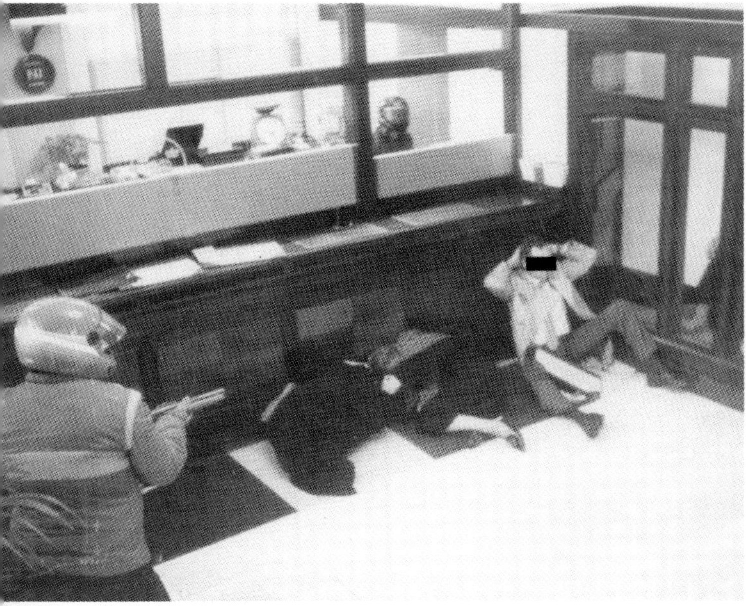

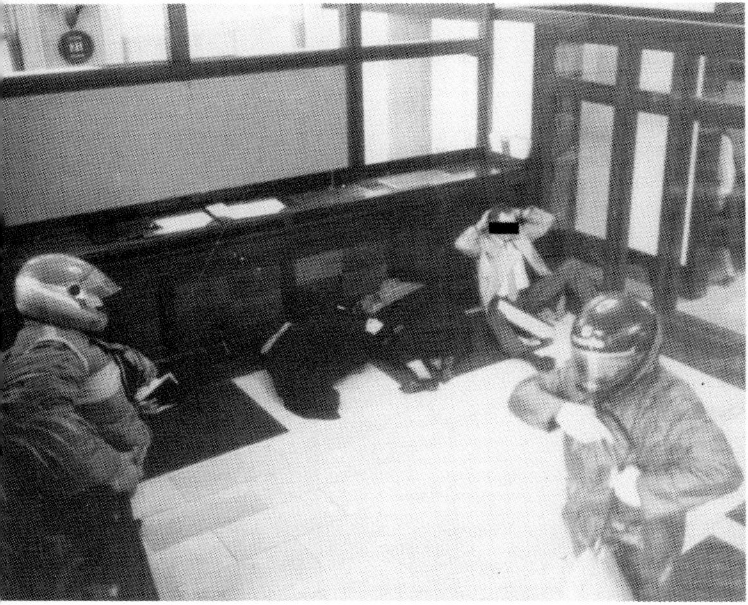

Above: Sitting with the 'enemy'. Richard Leach and I talking of this book. **Parkhurst**, Sept. 1992

Below: My favourite haunt and also my downfall-Whites Hotel.

too fast to live

of the problems I had faced in Cavendish Square.

*   *   *

The bank was situated on the ground floor of a large block and although some of its windows overlooked Curzon Street, its main entrance was in a small side street. To ordinary people this may seem irrelevant, but to a bank robber it is logistically very important that the entrance of a target is not exposed to pedestrians and traffic alike. A few seconds advantage often made the difference between success and failure, especially in an area like Mayfair where police patrols and diplomatic protection are very common.

I had targeted the bank a few weeks earlier and every time I was in the area I used to go there and buy some foreign currency in order to have an excuse to look at the security arrangements, staff, cash movements, etc.

I had also planned various alternative getaway routes. However, what was more important was that this was going to be my first robbery in England of a bank fully protected by reinforced glass. The public were separated from the staff side by those glass panels that are now common to most banks. I had studied two different techniques to overcome this problem and it was now time to put one of them into practice. The first of these techniques was applicable exclusively to Midland branches, therefore I concluded that it wasn't worth the effort as my aim was to 'patent' a technique that I could use with all the banks. The second option was definitely

valerio viccei

suitable for all banks as it was based upon a human factor instead of a technical one.

Like most banks this little branch had a reinforced door through which the employees could gain access to the other side. During my checks I had noticed that the same guy, always at the same time, used to come out through this door in order to reach the main entrance and shut the front door. This happened at about 3.39 pm and the guy then stayed next to the front door, now shut, until the last client was dealt with. Then he would walk back towards the other door, open it and go back to his business.

After careful planning I decided that I would walk into the bank at about 3.25 pm and wait by the counter next to the intercom door, acting like an ordinary client busy filling in some forms. As soon as the guy came through this door, I would deal with him.

* * *

I was riding a Honda bike with another man sitting behind me. I carried my Beretta handgun and he was carrying a sawn-off shotgun. We were both wearing crash helmets! I was also wearing an Acquascutum mac under which I hid a large nylon bag, secured to my body by reinforced string. My friend was dressed as a Pony Express courier.

I parked the bike just a few yards away from the main entrance and made sure that nobody could see it from inside the bank. The street was extremely quiet and there

too fast to live

was not a soul in sight. I was confident that everything would be fine and that my new technique would work the way I expected it to.

I told my friend to wait a little while before going into the bank and to do so only after I reached the till next to the intercom door. He could see me through one of the windows looking out on to the side street. I left my crash helmet on top of the bike seat and put on a hat and spectacles instead.

There were just six people queuing up in front of the only two working cashiers: the till that I was standing at was normally used as an information desk, thus I could take my time and pass totally unobserved. As soon as I leaned over a few forms collected from a dispenser, I noticed my partner coming through the front door. Although he was wearing a full-face crash helmet and biker gear, nobody seemed to pay any attention to him.

If the intelligence I had gathered over the past weeks was right, the man acting as porter should come out from the other side any minute now. The door was not more than two yards away from where I was standing and when I saw it opening, I moved swiftly towards it. Nobody was looking at me, not even my dumb ass of a partner! The timing was perfect. When the bank employee was almost face to face with me, I drew out my gun, pushed him backwards through the doorway and followed him through to the other side. It was even easier than I expected!

'I'm sorry, Sir, you're not supposed to come through this door. Do you mind going back, please?'

valerio viccei

The fool had not even noticed my gun and thought that I only wanted to talk to a member of the staff. As the door was still open, however, I couldn't take the risk of him yelling his head off as soon as he realised what it was all about. To make things worse, for some reason there was another employee right behind the man and this prevented me from pushing him further back and closing the door. Something had to be done!

I levelled my gun at his face and spoke very softly, almost in a whisper, 'Be calm and walk backwards. This is a robbery and I am not kidding. Just keep quiet, both of you. MOVE!'

Shock and fear struck the two guys immediately, but they did as they were told. I could now shut the door. Absurd as it may seem, nobody had yet noticed anything, not even my partner . . .

I was protected from the cashiers' side by wooden partition panels. In front of me there was only one lady, with her back to me, working on a computer screen. I softly told the 'porter' to hand me the keys he was carrying in his hand. I was not keen to re-live the Coutts' experience and the keys represented my way out. I ordered them to lie on the floor, adding that I was not going to hurt them unless they messed about. They relaxed immediately and smiled at each other; I don't know why, but I smiled too. Before I moved on I told them that my partner was on the other side and if they even tried to open the door, he would blow their heads off. They stopped smiling, but nodded nevertheless. It was at this point, while the two of them were sitting on

too fast to live

their asses and I was moving on all fours so as not to be seen by the cashiers, that the girl turned round and looked as though she was about to scream her head off.

'No, baby, don't do that or you're gonna be in trouble. Just keep calm.'

It worked and I could almost see the scream being swallowed down her windpipe, but then another girl, sitting next to her and clearly puzzled by her behaviour, decided to take a look at what was going on behind the wooden partition.

'You sit down too, darling. This is no joke.'

Everything seemed to be under control and it was now time for the serious business. One more warning to my four friends and I stood up. I reached for a catch on the other side of the partition panel and opened a section of it. I now found myself directly in front of the public, separated only by glass. Nobody seemed to understand what was going on: the cashiers were so surprised to see someone on the 'wrong' side that they stared dumbly at me. I grabbed the nylon bag and threw it at one of them.

'Fill it with all the cash. MOVE!'

I had to repeat it a couple of times as the man was too shocked to act, with the result that some of the clients realised I was no security guard.

I raised the gun towards them only to realise that some were already lying on the floor; I gestured to the others to do the same. Which they did.

But where was that son of a bitch of a partner?

I tried to ignore this worrying thought and shouted one more time at the cashier who was making a mess with the money. Half of it kept falling on the floor. I reached for the bag and finished the job myself. In a matter of seconds I had completed my task and quickly walked towards the door where the girls and the two men were still sitting motionless.

I opened the door and, before I left, I patted the 'porter' on the head: 'Next time watch more carefully, pal, there are plenty of bad men out there!'

At the same time I gave him back his keys and winked. He smiled again: he really was a nice fella. And now I wanted to know what the hell had happened to that idiot of a partner.

I looked around only to discover that the clown was lying on the floor together with the clients, his shotgun still inside the plastic shopping-bag. I kicked him in the butt and told him to get up. I was so gobsmacked I didn't know what to say.

Once we were on the bike I started calling him the worst names I could think of, only to be told that he had not seen me getting through the intercom door and that when I shouted 'Everybody on the floor!' his was an instinctive reaction.

I felt the best thing would be to dump him under a bus, but luckily for him there wasn't one about and anyway the fifty grand or so I was carrying could help me to forget the whole thing very quickly.

*   *   *

At the beginning of April 1987, soon after the Midland

too fast to live

robbery, I left for South America with Peter. We planned to spend a week or so in the north of Colombia, possibly in Santa Marta or Cartagena, and from there fly to Brazil and watch the Formula One Grand Prix in Interlagos. Somehow I got the dates wrong and we were still in Colombia when the Grand Prix took place. Nonetheless I loved the place. We were staying at the Hilton in Cartagena and everything was fantastic. Food, weather, cocaine and . . . women!

Peter left me quite soon. He did not speak or understand Spanish, and my sexual activity kept him out of the room for most of the time, day and night, when the hotel was fully booked and no other rooms were available. He left for Rio de Janeiro after a couple of weeks and that was a big mistake. Unbeknown to both of us, the Hilton Hotel hosted the yearly contest of Miss South America at just this time.

As soon as Peter left, the hotel filled with stunning ladies from all over South America, not all of them challengers for the title. Many were simply models or well-off young girls who wanted to witness such a glamorous event. I had the time of my life and, with pure cocaine at ten dollars per gram, I felt as though I could stay for ever.

I also met an extraordinary character named Budd. He was an oldish American, a tough nut and a great rogue. I never asked him what his job was, but he sort of ran the casino in Cartagena and was regarded by his employees and the hotel staff alike, as kind of a 'godfather'. He was a fantastic companion who drank

Pitia Colada as though it was mineral water for eighteen hours each day. I remember him fondly as one of a disappearing species — an old pirate.

After about three weeks I was running out of money and cursing myself for having brought with me only $10,000. I decided to spend my last few hundred dollars in the notorious city of Medellin. During my stay at the Hilton I had met a lovely girl called Gloria who was living there and I had promised her that before going back to London I would spend a few days with her. As it happened, I arrived in Medellin at the wrong time, as she was spending the weekend in the country with her boyfriend, but she arranged for a girlfriend to pick me up at the Intercontinental Hotel. She could not have sent a better substitute and I had a wonderful time.

Needless to say I ended up in bed with her the same evening and when Gloria came back I didn't make a secret of it. The only problem was to find the time and the energy to satisfy both.

Far too soon it was time to leave, but when the hotel bill was produced I almost choked! I did not have enough money left and although my ticket was already paid, there was no way I could settle the balance. It was a Friday so I couldn't have money sent from my numbered account in Switzerland. Besides, I was carrying a passport in a totally different name and would have had to offer too many explanations. Gloria and her friend offered to lend me some money, but my pride would not allow me to accept. I called a friend in London, but even though he was able to send the money, it would take four or five

too fast to live

days, at the very least, to reach me and my flight was just forty-eight hours away.

Finally I got hold of Peter who, by now, was back in London and asked him to buy an open ticket with KLM for me. After that, I called Eric, a very good friend in New York and arranged for him to deposit a thousand bucks in my name at one of the New York Intercontinental hotels and they would telex it to Medellin. Well, I thought I was safe, but plenty of trouble was still waiting for me.

An extremely kind and classy lady working for KLM in Medellin, Catalina Ochoa, literally falsified papers in order to get me a seat on the flight from Bogota to Miami and the connection with Delta Airlines to New York, where Eric was waiting for me. Everything was sorted out thanks to the kindness of friends and the marvellous people of Colombia — with one or two exceptions of course, one of whom I happened to meet at the international airport of Bogota.

After I checked out of the Tequendama Hotel, probably one of the largest and most luxurious hotels in all of South America, I asked a cab driver to take me to the airport. I was waiting to check in, when some son of a bitch managed to get my wallet out of my holdall including my phoney passport, my money and the tickets.

Needless to say I missed the flight and had to spend a couple of hours at the airport information centre, pursuing the impossible task of recovering at least my passport, as I knew only too well that I could already say goodbye to all Eric's money! However, there is a saying in

valerio viccei

my country that God's ways are eternal, therefore one should never despair.

After a while I happened to notice a man sitting on a chair. He was wearing American boots and a ten-gallon hat. He did not say a word and never even hinted that he might have had anything to do with the whole business. The man just sat there and kept asking about a key he had supposedly lost. He spoke in heavily accented American.

My intuition told me that he was there for a different reason. I listened to his accent; I analysed his body language as though my very life depended on it, and the more I did so the more I believed I was right. At last I approached him and, before he could say anything, I started telling him what I thought of Colombia and her lovely people, my sad incident notwithstanding. He replied that I was wrong and that they were, in fact, all thieves and liars who ought to be shot there and then!

I knew he was just testing me. I mentioned that being an Italian I knew what a bad reputation could do to a whole country, besides I did not feel resentment towards the chap who pinched my wallet. I wished him good luck and I only hoped he would return the passport and the tickets which were of no use to him and indispensable to me. He wished me luck and left with a big smile. Speaking in perfect Spanish for the first time, he said: 'Adios amigo! Buena suerte y buen viaje.' He was clearly Colombian!

Two hours later, while I was talking to the Italian Ambassador in Bogota and trying to accomplish the

too fast to live

impossible task of having my passport replaced, a phone call from the airport told us that my documents and flight tickets had been recovered under a telephone in the information centre. The operator said that it was the most unbelievable thing she could remember in her whole career. I thought of the man with the American boots and the large hat who had taken such a risk. Wherever you are, amigo, may God bless you and your country!

I had to rearrange my flight and the open ticket I had requested from Peter proved to be priceless. Twenty-four hours later I was at the arrival terminal of Kennedy Airport and Eric was there waiting for me.

I rested for a few days in New York and at the weekend I left for London, via Amsterdam. I checked in at Whites Hotel just one hour after landing at Heathrow. It was the beginning of May 1987.

CHAPTER 5

The 'Key' to the Vaults

The escape in St John's Wood was well behind me now and the weeks I had spent in Colombia had done me a lot of good. I did not feel under pressure any more and I thought the police might have decided I had left the country for good. I had not forgotten Latif and how he behaved during the tense deal regarding my safety deposit box. I even sent him a friendly postcard from South America, in which I thanked him for his co-operation and wished him well. I really meant it too!

★   ★   ★

Tamara was a very attractive Russian lady. Not young, by any means, but with a lovely body and plenty of

valerio viccei

experience. A mutual friend had introduced us after I had pestered him for weeks. The result was a stormy relationship. I did not know Tamara's source of income and I did not care, but rumours were that she had managed to make $100,000 by spending one single night with an Arab millionaire. She was definitely wealthy and had a magnificent flat near Victoria. She was also very well connected and a member of exclusive places like Annabel's and Tramp's. Although her body could well compete with a teenager's, she was a heavy drinker and drugs user and her attitude towards people in general was screwed up. She came across as bossy, arrogant and very, very possessive. I spent many nights a week with her, but also often disappeared for days at a time, seeing other girls as usual. Terrible arguments would break out but I mostly just laughed because, as I saw it, we were just two friends who happened to have sex together.

I had first met Tamara before I went to Colombia and when I came back I contacted her again and we went out for a meal. During the dinner I happened to mention that I might need to rent a safety deposit box somewhere and she said that a good friend of hers could be of some help as he was in that kind of business and was a very discreet person. My intuition came into play almost immediately and I asked her if, by any chance, the man was a Pakistani. She said yes, and I was certain that we were talking of the same person: Parvez Latifi.

Briefly I told her the whole story and the way he had prevented my friend's wife from getting the contents of my box. She just laughed and, sipping from a glass filled

too fast to live

with delicious Krug, she pointed at a little golden container hanging from a Cartier chain and hidden from view by my smart Missoni shirt. The little container contained cocaine! 'He must have thought your box was full of that stuff, darling, and wanted to clean it out himself,' she said with studied circumspection and added, 'He loves it!'

I bowed, as if to congratulate her for her deep knowledge of human nature, and filled her glass again with champagne. I remarked that it was a pity that I couldn't use the centre any more because of that incident. To my amazement she replied that this would not be a problem, as Latif also ran an even larger centre in Knightsbridge!

I said nothing, but my brain automatically opened a new 'file' with Parvez's name on it, and amazing prospects began to fill my imagination. The next day I went through Yellow Pages and found what I was looking for in a matter of seconds. I dialled the number and recognised his voice immediately. I had to play my hand carefully. I knew that the man was clever, and Tamara's comments made me believe that he could be ruthless as well. That was exactly what I needed of him.

I began: 'Mr Latif?'

'Yes. How can I help you, Sir?'

'Well, first of all I should apologise to you for my bad manners. I hope you have forgiven me and understood the pressure I was under.'

Silence from the other end of the line. I held my breath, thinking that I might have screwed everything up even before I started, then he spoke again. 'I am sorry, but I do not understand, Sir. Do you mind being a little more specific?'

This was exactly what I had hoped for and I was sure that he had already made the connection. I have a strong Italian accent and, in addition to that, I did not believe that clients threatened him every day. No, he was definitely fishing and that was a good sign.

'Mr Latif, I hope you did not mind me sending that silly postcard from South America, but I felt I had to apologise somehow.'

'Mr . . . Umberto! Is that correct?'

'Yes, that's the name.'

'And how are you, Sir?'

'Fine, thank you. Definitely much better than a few months ago. My doctor told me that carwash crossing in January is not too healthy a business and he suggested that Colombia with her Caribbean Sea was a much better cure for my bad sinuses.'

Thunderous laughter was the reply to my joke and I knew that I was on the right course. The conversation went on for a few more minutes and, when asked if I had managed to clear things up with the police, I purposely did not give an entirely satisfactory answer. I wanted to check his reaction.

'Oh, I see . . .' was all I got, which suited me fine and allowed me to introduce the main reason for my phone call. I asked him if, given the circumstances, he would be so kind as to give me some advice as to where I could rent a safety box. His reply would be of paramount importance to an idea I had been cultivating since my dinner with Tamara.

'I personally believe that we could provide you with better facilities than any other centre or bank in the City. As for discretion, I think that the unfortunate incident of a few months ago must have confirmed to you where our loyalty lies, Mr Umberto. I would certainly be prepared to handle all the necessary paperwork personally, if you wish.'

This man knew I was on the run; he must have read the newspaper reports about my background. He also knew that I was using a false name. All that notwithstanding, he was prepared to go along with this thing: why?

'Oh, that would be extremely useful, Mr Latif. How do you think it could be arranged?'

'No problem at all, my friend, as I am working here full time now. But if you could give me a little notice, I will make sure that I personally let you in through the back entrance. That side is very discreet and often offers easy parking facilities.'

'OK then, I shall come tomorrow morning at about ten o'clock and we can have a nice chat, if that is fine with you.'

'Yes, I am just making a note in my diary. See you tomorrow, and . . . have a nice day.'

I replaced the phone and took a long breath. I was also sweating — the pressure I had had to endure during the last five minutes was now taking its toll. I was in Whites Hotel and my room was just twenty yards away from the fresh green of Hyde Park. I opened the French window and my eyes sought the sun. It was a lovely day in May and I had the feeling that the implications of the phone call I had just made would change my life.

Vibes, you may say, old and battered vibes, but always dead right!

*   *   *

I had gone over and over my plan. I knew my speech and my act by heart, as though I was shooting a take with a movie director. I wore my gold Rolex and my custom-made gold and diamond chain. My clothes were casual, but designer goods and clearly identifiable. My Louis Vuitton photo-bag and my Patek Philippe keyring would be obvious. These are all items that speak for themselves and they would be as important as a gold credit card. I wanted to establish our boundaries from day one; Latif must feel that I had money to burn. An extremely wealthy bandit always has 'status', but it is his roughness and lack of class that worry 'straight' people. They give themselves away and make the latter feel uncomfortable.

I belonged to the upper classes by birth. I also knew how to exploit my resources — my education and my class — to the full! As well as this, I had an ace up my sleeve. When I dropped it on the table, the game would be over. My adrenalin was pumping, the excitement was building up and I loved this sensation as much as a night in bed with the wildest of my girlfriends.

*   *   *

too fast to live

It was five minutes before 10 am. Together with Peter, I was at the back entrance of the Knightsbridge Safe Deposit Centre. I carefully observed the surroundings and paid particular attention to a security video camera hidden in the intercom. The place was unnaturally calm and inspired confidence. I liked it. We were let in by Latif himself who clearly recognised Peter from St John's Wood, where he lived and was a popular fellow. He had a flat in the High Street, just above the Coffee Shop.

You must realise that walking so close to a vault in the wealthiest area of probably the wealthiest city in the world, is to me what walking inside the Louvre is to art fanatics. I could almost smell the treasure hidden a few yards below my feet. My predominant feeling was of over-powering excitement.

We sat in Parvez's smart office and the conversation was a bit awkward. The subject I feared most was my escape from the police but I somehow felt that it wouldn't be brought up by any of us, Latif included. After a short while, Peter made an excuse and left. I asked Parvez how business was. I also made enquiries about the availability of the boxes, prices and so on. He was very polite and professional, but I couldn't help noticing that all my 'accessories' were being carefully evaluated by eyes used to weighing people by their appearance.

He invited me to go downstairs, where the strong room was, to have a look at the security arrangements. Once in the vaults, I was shown the various box sizes and two rooms; one was the so-called 'viewing room' and the other an open storage for large objects: mainly sealed

valerio viccei

trunks, paintings, silverware and precious carpets. My eyes shone and my mind tried to absorb as many details as possible. I said that I was satisfied with the security arrangements and that of the four box sizes, the most suitable to my needs would be the medium one. A new lock was taken out of a sealed plastic container and its two keys handed over to me. Latif carefully removed a 'dummy' plastic lock from the steel door of the chosen box and replaced it with the proper one. I was fascinated and speechless: this man was in full control of an Aladdin's cave!

He explained to me that everything worked in exactly the same way as at the other centre and I should now insert my code-card in the computer slot and dial a six-digit figure. While I did this, he discreetly looked the other way. We left the basement and, by means of a short flight of stairs, reached ground level again. Once in his office I was requested to sign a contract in which, he stressed, I did not need to write any name or address. The box number was enough, as he would know to whom it belonged.

It was time to leave and I had not yet played my ace. Things were fine the way they were, but I couldn't suppress my own instinct and I had to follow it. I said that it had been extremely nice of him to handle things personally and this made me feel obliged to return his kindness.

'I know it might sound a bit excessive, but by giving me the chance to clear the other box, you saved me from unmentionable problems. Besides, we have a friend in

too fast to live

common, someone who speaks highly of you, Mr Latif.'

'Then you must call me Parvez, if you wish. And who is it, if I may ask?'

'Well, all I am going to say is that she is a lovely lady with whom I have a very close relationship and this obliges me to be a little discreet. Nevertheless I fully trust her judgement and I hope you will accept a little present from me, as proof of my gratitude. I know that I may be doing something very stupid, but I am a person who follows his own instinct and you will have to forgive me again.'

He immediately extended his arms, waving his hands, as if to prevent me from digging inside my Vuitton camera-equipment case, but I was determined and, to his amazement, I brought out a small cardboard box, in dimension no bigger than one and a half cubic inches. The logo of Avianca, the Colombian airway, was printed on it. I was a little tense and I hoped this was the right thing to do; on the other hand I knew that Tamara had told me the truth and I had to exploit this little advantage now. He was on the verge of protesting again when I placed the little box on his desk and got up from my chair.

'All I can say is that if I am wrong, just chuck it in the bin and forget the whole thing. Please.'

Curiosity took over; there was no way that he would let me go without checking the contents of this trifle, which looked very much like an over-sized matchbox. He looked at me still in puzzlement and at the same time pulled the two little flaps at the top of the box. When he lowered his head to have a look, his eyes almost popped out of their sockets.

'This can't be real!' is all he could say.

A solid rock of pure, shining cocaine, weighing at least ten grams, now sat on top of his leather diary. It was diamond-like and the artificial light of the room gave it a peculiar white colour: no wonder it is called snow!

Latif was now like a seduced lover and I could hardly blame him. He looked at this tiny alkaloid rock as though it were unreal and I wondered if it would not be safer to lock the door from inside. He seemed to read my thoughts and got up and promptly secured the office door. He looked at me again and this time he was smiling.

'It is a little early for this sort of thing, but I would not mind making an exception. Will you join me? By the way, I can't find the proper words to thank you; I only have seen stuff like this in the movies!'

I sat down again, pleased with my gamble. The sensation I had felt the previous day, while looking at the blue sky over Hyde Park, engulfed me once more. A line of that beautiful rock would transform it into pure exhilaration. I knew that I was going to love every single aspect of what I already considered my ultimate challenge to society.

* * *

In the days to come, I started using the centre more than I actually needed to, and I made sure that whenever

too fast to live

Parvez and I were together in his office, one of us would offer some cocaine to the other. This was a bond that I was determined to exploit fully and I also felt that he enjoyed my company and was extremely relaxed. He knew that he had nothing to fear from me.

We often went down to the vaults together and I used my box even when I had no reason to. I wanted him to wonder what my real activity was and why I needed to take out or replace the box contents so often. I couldn't help noticing that curiosity was taking its toll of him, whenever I took the plastic box out, he had to force himself not to come inside the viewing room with me. It was a psychological game and I was determined to play it very carefully.

* * *

It was already the third week of May and I had kept moving from one base to another with regular frequency. I was now staying opposite the Victoria Casino where I had rented a little flat.

I was not entirely certain about Parvez. I did not know if the time was ripe for my next move, and this was unsettling me. I had met him many times now and we had even had lunch together a couple of times. Our chats had become more informal and he had made it clear to me that his business was not as good as it could or should be, something I had realised myself from the low incidence of customers during my regular visits to the centre. This was bad news for him, but very good for me.

valerio viccei

I had given away some of my 'secrets' and he seemed to be pleased that I placed trust in him. Slowly, I felt that we were becoming good pals. I was now at a crucial point and I spent a lot of my time thinking about the Safe Deposit Centre, its security arrangements, its location and its treasures. I knew that it was burglar-proof and that night protection was total. During my chats with Parvez I had learned how most of the security devices worked; the centre was riddled with sensors and its walls were as thick as those of a dam. If I wanted to violate this gigantic safe, I had to find the right key and I had come to the conclusion that it had to be a very peculiar one. Technically speaking, the centre was a masterpiece of security, but behind every perfect machine there is a human being who has programmed it and who operates it. I would go after the human factor: always the weakest and most vulnerable spot.

CHAPTER 6

Down to Business

It was a nice day and I decided to go to Harrod's. After some shopping, I would pop in to see Parvez. The information I had obtained from him, plus my own attention to the minutest detail, had brought me to the end of the first stage of my plan. I must now proceed to Stage Two and although I had drafted two or three alternatives, the key question was 'Would Parvez co-operate with me?'

Apart from Peter, who vaguely knew my ambition from the very start, nobody suspected what I was after. I had to talk to Parvez or everything would be pointless. I had made this decision but I knew I had to avoid too direct an approach. We met for lunch in a restaurant a few yards away from the centre and I chose a very quiet table. The nearest customers were out of earshot and I acted a little suspiciously on purpose. I wanted to know if Parvez felt uneasy or curious. I asked him if, in all honesty, the financial situation of his business was as bad as he had told me a few weeks earlier, or if I was right in assuming it was now much worse.

He replied that it was very bad and that unless a large injection of cash was obtained, it would be a matter for the Official Receiver very soon. He said all this without lifting his eyes from his plate and a little too quickly. It was now my turn to say something and I could feel him eager for my next words.

'Look, Parvez, we don't know each other very well and you may think that I am out of order asking these questions about your business, but I would like to help you. Unfortunately, I am not a businessman, nor do I have a magic wand, but . . .' and here I intentionally wolfed down a big lump of fillet steak, leaving my sentence unfinished.

He was now looking at me like an enchanted kid watching a magician. Enough, I thought.

'. . . but I have quite a large amount of cash available and many friends who are in the same position. We are not in an entirely orthodox business, but who is nowadays?'

'Oh, I see! It is nice of you, Gigi, but there is not a lot I could offer in return. I am just a junior partner of the enterprise and debts already run into hundreds of thousands.'

'Is it that bad, Parvez?'

'Yes, I am afraid it is . . . and it is getting worse every week.'

'No. Well, if you had the right insurance, it looks to me that the best thing that could happen to it would be a burglary or a robbery!'

I said this laughing aloud and avoiding eye contact. I did not want him to know if what I had said was just a joke or some sort of subtle advice. The bait was there and the ball lay in his court. It was more than enough for one day.

He laughed too, but I felt that there was tension in it. I did not expect any sort of commitment there or then, but I hoped that the subject wouldn't be dropped completely.

'Sometimes I can't help cursing the place for being so secure. What we advertise is supreme security and this must discourage even the toughest of villains. How can I blame them?'

It was now my turn to laugh at his joke, but I noticed the message he was trying to deliver. I felt I could take the matter a little further without revealing too much.

'Well, it is undoubtedly a very safe place, but I know people who would have no problem whatsoever in bypassing all the security arrangements and cleaning out most of the boxes. Believe you me!'

'Do you really know such characters?'

'I am not saying that it would be an easy thing, but, as we are being theoretical, and as I keep a box here, I have taken a look at the premises from the other side of the game and I have spotted some weak points. That's all.'

I now felt that I had said enough for one day. I wanted him to muse over the whole conversation calmly and in his own time. He could interpret it the way that suited him best.

I changed the subject then and our chat became little more than gossip about the attributes of the waitress who had been serving our table. After coffee, Parvez handed a very small paper envelope over to me and I did not need to ask what was inside. I headed for the toilet instead and drew out a crisp fifty-pound note. A line of cocaine would help my digestion and, more important, would leave him to think about what we had said. We parted outside the restaurant with a smile and a warm handshake.

In the meantime I had another project to complete.

After robbing the Midland Bank I had plenty of English cash and foreign currency, but what I had needed most before my trip to Colombia was American dollars.

Through my Swiss Bank I bought $10,000, but when I asked the cashier for small denomination notes, she apologised, saying that they had none. In Colombia the average monthly wages of a hotel receptionist were the equivalent of 150–200 US dollars, and it is obvious that carrying 100-dollar bills would make a person a very likely victim of robbery. I decided to change some of the notes in high street branches of the various British banks. To my surprise the cashiers seemed to be reluctant to accept dollars, as though the possibility of them being forged was more probable than for the other currencies.

In the end, I asked a cashier if he could tell me where

too fast to live

I could find an American bank. I was told that American Express branches would have no qualms about handling the exchange. After sweating over the directions I received, I ended up in an American Express branch, located on the ground floor of a building in Mount Street. It looked like a travel agency and I thought I was in the wrong place. I was on the point of leaving when I asked one of the staff if there was any chance of buying small denomination US notes. To my astonishment, this pretty girl told me that all I had to do was go downstairs to the basement and ask the cashiers.

After three flights of stairs I found myself in front of a ten-foot-long counter with armoured glass panels that almost reached the ceiling. On the right side of the room there were some chairs and a little desk, while on the left there was a door, protected by a combination lock. Through this door the employees working on the ground floor had access to a fairly large office where I spotted a huge safe. From this office, a further door led to the cashiers' side of the counter. They looked smug and well satisfied with their security. Ha!

After half a dozen clients were dealt with, a pleasant girl asked if she could help me. I briefly told her my problem and, after rummaging inside a couple of drawers, she said that she had only a few small denomination dollar bills.

I enquired if she would mind asking her colleague too, as it was very important to me. I also added that I had been trying all morning with other banks. She was very kind and did exactly what I asked her! While this exchange took place I was standing opposite to her, at an angle which did not give me the opportunity to look inside her desk, but this did not apply to the other cashier's desk. In order to get a better view, I discreetly stretched my neck like a giraffe and, when the other girl opened her own drawer wide, my eyes almost popped out of their sockets. Large bundles of English and foreign currencies were neatly stacked inside. We were talking serious money here!

I was not yet completely satisfied with what I had seen, and when the first girl apologised again, I took out of my holdall $10,000, stacked in hundreds, saying: 'Why is it that in this city nobody has any bloody dollars?'

The girl was clearly taken aback by my outburst and, perhaps out of wounded pride, she grabbed two large wads of US dollars saying: 'Sir, this is 20,000 dollars, but we have no small denomination notes!'

I left the place as happy as a little kid who has just had a good look at the toy he is going to get for Christmas. This little branch was already mine. The 20,000 bucks I saw told me a lot about the amount of cash I would find there.

It was therefore unavoidable that when I decided to pull off one more job, my mind already focused on the Knightsbridge Safe Deposit Centre, the American Express branch in Mount Street was the perfect choice. Good money and very little risk!

I went in a couple more times and checked the place inside out. No video cameras and apparently no security staff; but the 20-inch gap between the reinforced glass

too fast to live

panels and the ceiling was still there.

Coutts had taught me a tough lesson and I now spent a great deal of time checking the counter and ceiling for all possible grooves. The prospect of being squashed against the ceiling like a fly wasn't too attractive. Everything looked fine to me, especially when I happened to be there when one of the ground floor employees walked into the large office in the basement. She just dialled a five-digit figure and the door security lock was released at once.

Obviously, it was my intention to get to the other side of the counter through this wonderful gap, but it wouldn't be easy. Firstly, I would have to climb up on to the particularly narrow wooden shelf used by clients to fill in forms and cheques. Secondly, I would have to do this while holding my gun, wearing a full-face crash helmet and with a Pony Express carrier bag strapped to my chest. On top of all this, such an operation would be hampered by the closeness of the perpendicular glass panels, which did not offer any holds. I would, in fact, have to stand on the narrow counter ledge, jump up, grab the top of the panels, swing my body through the gap and down to the floor fast enough to prevent the cashiers getting away through the side door. It was definitely a very tricky business.

In the end I decided that one of the chairs could help me to overcome most of the problems. I would use it as a springboard to jump on to the counter, and, from there, swing over the glass panels!

valerio viccei

*   *   *

On the afternoon of 22 May 1987 I was riding an old Honda along the busy streets of the West End. Another man rode pillion. Both of us were armed and wearing full biking gear.

We had left Grosvenor Square behind and, after covering a hundred yards of South Audley Street, had arrived in Mount Street. The American Embassy, with all its massive security apparatus, was two hundred yards away. I could feel my partner's tension increasing by the minute. Nevertheless, the money was needed to fund the Knightsbridge Safe Deposit Centre business.

As usual, I dropped my partner off a few yards from target and then parked the bike opposite American Express. As agreed, I went straight in and headed for the basement.

There were a few customers at the counter and I decided to sit down on a chair and wait for a while. In the meantime I started toying with some forms and a pen. By a lucky coincidence, as soon as the last client was served, my partner reached the bottom of the stairs and nodded at me, as if to say that everything was fine. He stayed there.

As though it was the most natural thing in the world, I calmly got hold of one of the chairs and walked towards the counter. I laid the chair against it. Nobody seemed to pay attention to what I was doing. Perhaps they thought I was trying to be funny. As if to confirm this, I walked backwards a few yards and then, suddenly, I ran towards

too fast to live

the chair again, jumped on it and from there on to the narrow section of the counter.

The cashiers were too shocked to react and when they came to terms with what was happening it was too late: I had reached the edge of the partitions and a gun had appeared in my hand. They froze!

The only one who didn't was a chap in the adjoining room, from whom I was only separated by ordinary glass. He had reached for a phone and was dialling. At the top of my voice I shouted, 'Freeze!!! You mother fucker, get that phone down or you are history!' and I pointed my gun at him. It did the trick and the lad dropped the phone as though it were red hot. I literally crash landed on the other side of the counter, making a lot of noise, and this awoke one of the cashiers from her state of shock! She started to scream and all my attempts to calm her down failed. I thought, 'They must be hearing this even in the American Embassy!'

I started filling the nylon bag with the money and bundles of 'virgin' American Express travellers cheques. I knew that I was running out of time and that soon half the London cops and anti-terrorist Rambos would be rushing towards the bank. I opened the intercommunicating door and quickly crossed the nearby office where all the employees were sitting quietly. I got entangled in a struggle with the lock and made a girl get up to help me open the door. I had the gun in my right hand, the bag in my left. I cursed aloud because of the inconvenience and I heard someone giggling in the background. I couldn't help laughing myself and gave the joker the finger. My partner

valerio viccei

must have been shitting himself. I couldn't see him on the ramp. He was upstairs in a totally empty office. Outside, all the employees were gathering on the pavement. I quickly jumped on the bike and we left the area.

Two minutes later we were in South Molton Street. I parked the Honda under a hidden archway and, after taking off our crash helmets and overalls, we headed for New Bond Street tube station which was just twenty yards away. All was fine and the coast was clear. Half an hour later I was in my flat opposite the Victoria Casino, counting the money. It was quite a lot, there was over $100,000 worth of 'virgin' American Express travellers cheques. These would be my bait for the Knightsbridge job.

I picked up the telephone and dialled a familiar number. As soon as a male voice replied, I said, 'Hi Parvez, it's me. I have very good news for you. We had better talk as soon as possible. See you in an hour at the Centre.'

*   *   *

'I am resolved on an enterprise which . . .
has no precedent and which, once complete,
will have no imitator.'
(Jean-Jacques Rosseau)

Knightsbridge was bustling with activity, as usual, and tourists milled around aimlessly, enjoying a late but sunny afternoon. Harrods was just behind me. I was wearing

too fast to live

my extremely bright designer shell-suit and snow-white Nike trainers. Anyone would think I was one of the large number of foreign shoppers crowding the pavement.

About an hour after the phone call I had left the flat and hailed a cab outside the Cumberland Hotel. I was carrying my Vuitton holdall and inside it I had neatly stashed all the cash taken from the American Express, the travellers cheques and the two weapons. I had also disassembled the shotgun and put it in a little nylon bag. I knew the meeting with Parvez was going to be crucial. Today I would find out what his real aims were. The rest would be a formality.

I reached the Centre very quickly despite the traffic and the security guard at the main entrance, John Fitzpatrick, said hello. He was a big man with a soft Irish accent and he knew that I was a friend of Parvez. He was relaxed and smiled as did Justine, one of the Centre's female staff and very, very pretty indeed. Parvez was clearly excited and I could tell that he had had some cocaine very recently, as his eyes were blinking too much and his hands were restless. He came towards the door to welcome me and we greeted each other like old pals. As soon as we were in his office, he locked the door, and smiling, asked me: 'So, my friend, have you won the lottery, or have you struck oil in Texas?'

'More or less,' I replied taking my sunglasses off. Only my eyes smiled, the tone of my voice was deadly serious and this had an immediate impact on him. He knew that I had come to talk business.

I carried on: 'Parvez, do you remember during our

lunch in the restaurant next door that you mentioned that some associates of yours could easily transfer money from one country to another, bypassing all the regular channels and bank regulations?'

'That's correct.'

'I have been thinking about it recently and I am wondering if, by any chance, these gentlemen are interested in, how shall I say it, "unsigned" American Express travellers cheques. A lot of them.'

'I do not understand, Gigi: what do you mean when you say "unsigned"? Whenever you buy travellers cheques they must be signed straightaway and countersigned when you use or cash them. Everybody knows that!'

'Hmmmm, let's say that these particular travel cheques have not been bought.'

'Are you saying that they are forged?' he asked with a note of surprise in his voice.

'No, Parvez, they are good as gold. Actually they come from a London American Express branch, but the only problem is that they have somehow been "lost" by the cashiers. Do you get it?'

'No, I honestly don't. And I want to emphasise that if there is anything wrong with them, just say so and let's talk about it as there is a solution to everything, my friend.'

'OK, say that a few hours ago someone visited this branch in the West End and left the premises with a bag full of cash and over $120,000 worth of blank travellers cheques, all of which are still in their sealed envelopes.

too fast to live

What would you say?'

'When can I have them? That's what I would say.'

I roared with laughter and I got up off my chair to shake his hand, saying 'That's a good businessman, Parvez! My congratulations.'

I made it clear to him that they were all available and that if he or his associates were really interested, we had only to agree a price. The sooner they were disposed of, the better and the safer. I added that, considering our particular relationship, I was prepared to give him a huge commission and that he could even keep all the proceeds of the deal in order to inject cash into the company's account. I pointed out that I did not need money at that moment and he could give it back to me later on. I did not expect interest, nor any written commitment from him. A simple handshake would do.

He could hardly believe what I had just told him, and for a second, I had the feeling that he might even refuse my proposal on the basis that it was clearly too generous. The feeling did not last too long.

We talked the subject over for a while, but I had the feeling that his knowledge of illegal business was more a pretence than anything else. That notwithstanding, the moral issue of the whole deal was never brought up. I recalled Tamara's words and smiled at the man now sitting in front of me, wearing a Savile Row suit and looking after his customers' treasure. I was now sure that, had I not managed to escape from the police, he would have cleaned my box out whenever the time was right. This thought gave me quite a buzz and I decided to carry on with my plan.

I had observed him carefully and paid great attention to whatever he said with regard to the travellers cheques and other petty tricks, like multiple share applications and VAT dodging. In Italy my nickname was, and still is, 'the Wolf' because of my predatory instinct. I could smell his pretence and I was prepared to hunt my prey down. This man was not interested in the cheques, he most probably wouldn't know how to cash them if they had been bought straight from the bank.

No, he was after my true occupation and my connections: we were playing the same game and for the first time I felt that even our target might be the same. The time was ripe, I felt it in my bones, and this was a chance I couldn't afford to let go: it was now or never.

'Look, Parvez, I understand that this is just a little deal and it would hardly help you to put this business right so I apologise for mentioning it to you, but I wanted to make sure that we spoke the same language; I hope you understand that. What I am saying is, why don't we think of a way to make serious money out of our mutual resources and activities, without fucking about and wasting each other's time?'

'Is there one?'

'Well, I can interpret what you have just said as a question or, more likely, as an answer. Which one of the two, Parvez?'

He couldn't suppress a smile and, shaking his head slowly, he reached for his cigarettes: 'I knew you were ruthless, Gigi, but I am glad to see that you are extremely clever as well. Right, let's hear what you have got in mind.'

I talked for a good half hour, during which we were interrupted a few times by the staff and some phone calls, to which he paid very little attention. He was alert and a little tense. An extremely risky operation might save him: a simple mistake and he would be ruined. I did not push too hard and my idea was pretty vague. It was his availability I was after and I thought that I had it already. The next move would tell me.

He did not interrupt me, but just kept nodding and smiling from time to time. I was convinced, however, that he would try to make me believe he had a better and less risky idea himself. It is typical of all crooked businessmen to consider themselves smarter than the real predators. Latif was no exception.

I mentioned that breaking into the Centre was my dream and that if I could count on his co-operation it would be more than feasible. The technical details were still in the gestational stage, thus he could object to the validity of some of my theories, which I would accept.

All of a sudden he said that a friend of his owned a Safe Deposit Centre in Karachi and that he would be ready to make a deal with us. The place had no up-to-date security protection, no video cameras and no silent alarm system. The only surveillance consisted of two armed guards who belonged, in every meaning of the word, to this friend of his. The fortunes hidden in there, he said, were incalculable and a hundred times more than those under our feet.

valerio viccei

I gave it some thought, but thought of it as a further screen, the last defence I had to break through before his capitulation was total. I replied that this would imply too many logistical problems and that a gang of Europeans in Karachi would stick out like a sore thumb. Besides, if we were to be caught, they would cut my dick off.

I suggested that we broke off our conversation for a while so that the staff didn't get suspicious, but the real reason was a different one and I thought that my next move would finally defeat his resistance or, better still, would give him the excuse he was looking for. I therefore asked him if he minded coming down to the vaults with me as I had to replace something in my box and get some coke out of it. He got up from his chair at once and unlocked the door. We left together.

Unlike my previous visits to the vaults, Parvez was right next to me even when I opened my box, but the large plastic container in which I kept all my stuff prevented him from seeing what was in it. I started walking towards the viewing room and, as we were the only two people there, I invited him to follow me inside. As soon as I closed the door, I told him not to be shocked by what he was going to see as I wanted to show him that I meant business, and that what I had said in his office was true.

I placed the grey plastic box on the table and opened it. Latif couldn't help seeing that it was filled with bundles of brand new fifty-pound notes, all neatly stacked and still in the bank-sealed plastic bags. His expression changed. I then opened the Vuitton bag and took out

too fast to live

bundles of travellers cheques, which I piled up on the table. Finally I took out about £100,000 in various currencies, clearly proceeds of the robbery committed a few hours earlier. As I expected, at this point, his jaw dropped. I laughed aloud and patted him on the shoulder. At the same time I replaced the handgun in the box, making sure that he saw perfectly well what I was doing.

I took some cocaine out of a plastic film container, and amid his protests, handed it over to him. I replaced everything in the box, leaving out only ten thousand in cash, which I put in my Vuitton bag. I replaced the box in its container, secured the lock and smiled at Parvez, but he was too shocked to say a single word.

*   *   *

A few days had gone by since my last visit to the Centre and I had the feeling that Parvez would have been thinking intently about what I had told him and what he had seen. There was no way he could contact me and this would make things pretty tense for him. I saw no reason to rush; I wanted to be sure that he had plenty of time to think things over.

It was early on a Friday afternoon when I called him and he suggested that we met later on at the Centre. About 6 pm would be ideal, he added, as at about that time all the staff left the premises. Only the security guards would be there and we could have a quiet chat. I said that that was fine with me.

I could tell before he opened his mouth that he had

valerio viccei

finally made up his mind. There was a different light in his eyes. He would co-operate fully and would enjoy every single moment of what we were going to do. I might be wrong, but I would have bet everything I had that he was not going to waver.

We sat in his office for quite a long time. Once he had given me full assurance that he was now ready to go along with my plan, I shook his hand and made it clear that there was no going back from this decision. Now I could finally relax. For the first time in my life I had in my pocket a man who was in charge of an Aladdin's cave. I might be mad, I might be an arrogant son of a bitch, but I knew that I would pull it off. Nothing was going to stop me!

I had no clear plan in my mind yet, but that was irrelevant; what I needed was detailed information, anything to do with security, alarms and clients. I made it clear to him that this thing would happen and if he thought I was just playing games, he was making a serious mistake. I also added that our agreement would include the following:

I would pick a team of people whom he would never meet.

On the day of the robbery I would leave the Centre with all the loot.

He would not know where I would be staying after the job.

Finally, the cash obtained from the sale of whatever I found in the boxes would be divided into three parts: one part would go to the team of helpers, while the other

too fast to live

two would be divided equally between me and him.

He smiled and said that it was more than he had hoped for. I left relieved. I had just broken the 'code' of one of the safest combination locks in the world and the prospects were staggering.

I spent a whole week meeting with Parvez and writing memos, synopses of plans and lists of the most unusual equipment you could think of. I drew a huge map of the Safe Deposit Centre, memorised every detail and checked the location of all the police stations within a mile radius. Maps of the Knightsbridge area were now spread liberally all over my flat, only being locked up in the wall safe when I left for a quick meal, usually at Wolfe's. I was totally taken over by the whole thing. I slept very little and took no time off, but loved it more than any other thing I had ever done.

I was alone and I could rely on nobody else. Peter was the only one who knew what I was after but he asked me no questions and I told him very little. I mentioned that I was considering a simple role for him. According to the latest plan I had drafted, I was thinking of letting him into the Centre only after I had secured the premises and when the whole place was under my control. Like some of the others I would contact in the weeks ahead, he probably didn't believe that I was going to pull it off, which was why he accepted my offer with just a nod and a simple smile.

It was a huge, unbelievable task and I knew only a few people who could help me during this delicate phase. Unfortunately, they were also known to the police and I didn't want to spoil my marvellous brainchild if they should be under surveillance because of their own activities. This was an operation that I would have to plan carefully from scratch and entirely on my own. It would be impossible to describe my state of mind during the first two weeks of the planning. My brain was totally clogged by the multitude of data it was fed, the various options it had to consider; my concentration was total, my dedication close to manic obsession. I was totally enchanted.

I was still seeing Helle from time to time but, obviously, she knew nothing about the business. We often spent weekends together but she didn't ask any questions about what I did when I was on my own.

During this period I was also in touch with a few people whom I had met soon after I came back from Colombia, and with others whom I had known for some time. One of these was David, a man in his late forties, who was extremely funny and good company. He enjoyed a few lines of cocaine, knew a lot of young ladies and, despite his age, behaved like a youngster. I felt at ease with him. Before I had left for Colombia, just two months earlier, I had spent a few days at his place as a guest and that had brought us a little closer. I thought I could trust this man, and he proved to be as good as gold.

Through David and an Italian friend of mine, I also met Steve who was in his thirties and had a beautiful, but bitchy wife. They were not in love with each other any longer, but they were definitely in love with cocaine.

With the plan taking over most of my life by now,

too fast to live

when I was not seeing Helle, I spent what little free time I had with these friends. Cocaine and ladies were always available and, generally speaking, I had a very good time, but as the Knightsbridge project began to occupy more and more of my mental and physical resources, I had to slow down a little.

I kept up my meetings with Parvez and, one evening, he asked if I would like to go out for dinner with him and his girlfriend. He said that it would be nice if I could bring a female friend with me. I considered the risks of this promising evening out; I was extremely curious and I wanted to meet the woman who was living with him. I thought that I ought to find out what sort of person she was, how intelligent and how nosy. How much could she interfere with my plans and what hold did she have on Parvez? His attitude towards women worried me, but as long as it didn't interfere with Knightsbridge that remained his problem.

I said that I would love it and would bring Helle along. The two of them had met briefly at the other Safe Deposit Centre in St John's Wood, and she was the only girl I knew who wouldn't ask silly questions.

I offered to choose the place and make the booking. He objected for a while, but in the end I managed to overcome his resistance. I opted for 11 Park Walk, just off the Fulham Road. I believed it to be the best Italian restaurant outside Italy. It was smart and exclusive but not too pretentious. The food was beautiful and the service excellent. I had been a regular customer there for over a year, and was on friendly terms with the two owners and

valerio viccei

all the waiters, thus I knew that we would have the best table and a lovely evening.

It was a Saturday evening and the restaurant was full as usual. Some of the men wore tuxedos, while most of the ladies were in bright evening dresses. The atmosphere was very pleasant; everybody was smiling and prolonged laughter resounded. I noted some very classy necklaces and beautiful diamond rings, while gold Rolex and Cartier wrist watches were de rigeur.

In my country a similar place would have been protected by armoured doors and armed security; here the glass door stood wide open and the receptionist was a pretty, ever-smiling young lady. I grinned at the comparison.

Helle and I sat on a small leather sofa to the left of the pretty bar counter. We sipped fine champagne and watched the privileged clients, trying to imagine what they might think of us. They probably assumed that we were just like them, extremely wealthy and without worries!

My attention was mainly focused on the stunning ladies who glided around with studied provocation. They certainly knew how to promote their beautiful bodies. Helle kept pulling the left sleeve of my jacket to interrupt my train of thought, but she knew what I was like and mostly just laughed it off.

As usual I pulled funny faces and widened my eyes at the ones with big boobs and beautiful, uplifted bums. This usually generated more laughter than embarrassment, and one of the two owners, Salvatore, shook his head and said aloud: '*Gigi, sei proprio incorregibile!*'

I raised my glass and smiled at him. He did the same and comically widened his eyes as a 'bombshell' walked by. We both laughed and Helle covered her face with both hands, pretending deep shame.

Parvez was a little late and I wondered if he was having trouble parking. I was still thinking about this when a tall, very attractive and smartly dressed young lady walked through the front door. She seemed to be on her own. She was wearing a black evening dress that emphasised her large breasts and barely half-covered them. Her shoes were smart. The heels were too high as she was already very tall, but her long, shapely legs gained further advantage from this, making the way she walked towards the bar very provocative. Many eyes followed her; mine and Salvatore's were definitely four of them!

She was blonde, her long hair was cut just above those beautiful boobs and clearly the result of some coiffeur's hard, professional work. Only her jewellery struck me as a little inexpensive, as did her watch, but the rest was perfect. Like most of the men in the restaurant, I was wondering what lucky bastard was laying her. Needless to say, Helle had almost pulled my sleeve off. Then in came Parvez.

He walked through the door and saw me almost immediately, but he kept looking round as though he was looking for someone else. Then he crossed towards the bar. The stunning blonde was his girlfriend!

She spelled trouble, I could tell immediately as soon

valerio viccei

as we were introduced to one another, and I felt that this was going to be a highly charged evening. Were it not for the very peculiar nature of my partnership with Parvez I would have loved the inevitable clash of personalities which lay ahead, but, under the circumstances, I was going to have to show some restraint. Well, I would try my best.

My first impression wasn't wrong. Pamela came across immediately as very spoiled and unfriendly. She was obviously used to marking her own territory from the very start whenever males were around. I felt a bit uncomfortable for Helle and far more for poor Parvez, but there was no way I was going to endure an evening with a beautiful but unfriendly egocentric dictating the rules. There was no mistake about it. I was her target and the other two were soon relegated to simple bystanders with virtually no part in the conversation. I didn't like it; I didn't like it one little bit!

The waiters were busy preparing our table and we decided to sip some champagne at the bar. Once again I had been introduced as Gigi. I really hated that stupid name. She obviously found it amusing and marked me down as a wop. The English are such snobs sometimes!

Helle said nothing, she just stared at the ceiling from time to time and, if unobserved, mildly shook her head. Women foresee trouble the way cats can smell dogs and she knew I wouldn't take any shit from this character!

Parvez, poor chap, looked like a French poodle whose mistress was not pleased with it.

I was tempted to ask the young lady if she would

too fast to live

mind helping me make a phone call and then, once we were alone, tell her what a pain in the ass she was and kindly advise her to stop spoiling our evening. Helle must have noticed what was going through my mind as she gently pinched the back of my hand and smiled as if to encourage me to calm down.

While I was simmering down a little, I studied Pamela carefully. Suddenly, I realised that I knew her! I had seen this flash blonde before and more than once. But where, when and with whom? For once my photographic memory let me down. The memory was there, I could sense it, and my feeling was that the information would be useful to me somehow.

Things improved slightly and I tried not to take much notice of her odd behaviour. I found myself wondering about the life Parvez had to endure with such an unsettling young lady, and I also wondered why he had never mentioned her before. I was tempted to ascribe this to shyness and to a justified unwillingness to disclose the obvious failure of their relationship. It made me feel uncomfortable nevertheless.

With that natural lack of tact that I am capable of showing under the most inappropriate circumstances, I tried to discover a little more about 'them' by means of an apparently innocent remark.

'Parvez, I think that your girlfriend is a very nice person and an extremely good-looking young lady. Congratulations.'

'Yes, Pamela is a lovely girl. Thank you, Gigi.'

Parvez smiled, but I detected uneasiness in his

expression. As if to confirm this, the sound of a fork dropping heavily on a plate made him flinch.

'Why do you keep telling people that I am your girlfriend, Parvez?'

'Oh, come on now, Pam...'

'Shut up and try to be truthful with your friends. You idiot!'

Now, let me tell you something: I love women and I could not live without them. I may sometimes be an arrogant son of a bitch, but I would never physically hurt a woman, no matter what. Since my marriage I had not even raised my voice to a woman. I couldn't stand arguments any more; if they ever surfaced, it meant that it was time to part. Nonetheless, I would never allow any woman to speak to me like that. I was first angry, then surprised and shocked.

Before I said anything I took my time, slowly sipped some champagne and then wiped my lips with an immaculate napkin.

'Look, Pamela, he never told me anything. It was my assumption and if it was a wrong one, I am the one who should be reproached. In fact, Parvez and I have never talked about you. I give you my word,' I told her.

'It doesn't make any difference to me. He should have told you the truth in the first place and that would have avoided embarrassment to everybody but he never learns.'

'Anyway, I apologise, Pamela, OK?' Turning towards Parvez, I slowly added: 'Parvez, your friend is a nice, good-looking lady. Congratulations.'

I thought that this would settle the dispute and bring

too fast to live

a note of humour, but I was wrong. She wouldn't let it go.

'Gigi, are you taking the piss?'

'What did you say?'

'I asked if you are taking the piss.'

'Look, my English isn't too good, Pamela. I don't understand the meaning of such an expression. Do you mind explaining it in simpler words?'

My tone was not friendly, nor teasing any more and I hoped she was clever enough to realise it.

Luckily for everybody, she just shook her head and refilled her glass, but the atmosphere was pretty tense and nobody spoke for a while. What a fabulous night out!

Once dinner was over Helle and I were invited back to their place but, after the trauma I had had to endure already, I didn't feel like it. But my addiction to a challenge was taking over and I hesitated. Helle, prevented from pulling my sleeve again because it would be too obvious, started to kick me under the table and I gave in.

I was intrigued, nevertheless, Pamela's 'act' was just an unsophisticated technique intended to attract my attention. As far as I was concerned, her boobs and her beautiful bum had already done the trick, but some women have a tendency to overkill, and she, apparently, was one of them.

As soon as they were out of earshot, Helle said: 'I know what's going to happen. I know you too well. She's your favourite kind of woman, isn't she?'

I just laughed and told her she was mad, but we both knew she was right!

valerio viccei

The evening out was quickly forgotten, but the lady had succeeded in arousing my curiosity and I found myself thinking about her more often than I wanted to. Helle was right as usual; I fancied this beautiful woman.

I tried to concentrate on Knightsbridge. There was a huge amount of work to be done and this kept me really busy for most days and several nights. I continued to meet Parvez on a regular basis and a couple of times he invited me home for a drink. I knew I should decline, but she would be there and I was eager to find out what her attitude was going to be this time. Besides, a serious question was gnawing at me: 'Did she know anything?'

Such a frightening possibility made my spine shiver. I had asked Parvez a few times when his guard was down, but the man seemed almost offended by my question. He denied it so categorically that I felt I had to apologise to him.

I also asked him, very frankly, if there was any particular reason why she was so unfriendly towards me, but he simply smiled, saying that she was much worse with his Pakistani friends. Whenever they were around she just walked away or treated them so badly that they felt compelled to leave as soon as possible.

Another evening out was planned and this time I wanted to play it cool. I decided not to take Helle with me and thought I might take along an extremely flash and provocative young lady with whom I was having a relationship, mainly to make Pam feel uneasy, but this could easily backfire and I did not need further aggro from her. I would go on my own!

too fast to live

As it turned out, this was an option I did not have and I found myself paired with Parvez's sister. I had never met her before but she seemed to be a pleasant lady. Although she was very quiet, she was good company and extremely polite. I found her attractive as well and I would have been a little more forward were it not for the fact that she was Parvez's sister.

Anyway, the four of us went to Tramp's.

The place was crammed with beautiful people, as usual, but in the end we managed to find a nice table and ordered a bottle of champagne. I don't particularly like clubs and I don't feel very comfortable when I am surrounded by beautiful and provocatively dressed ladies. I can't stop turning my head around and making comments. I feel like a kid in a sweet shop and this doesn't go down too well with the ladies with whom I am spending the evening. Pamela was no exception and we had one of our usual heated arguments, with the result that she refused to talk to me for the rest of the time we spent there.

Afterwards the four of us were jammed into Pam's little Renault. She sat in the front, next to Parvez who was at the wheel. His sister lived in a smart block of flats very close to the Edgware Road, so the trip was very quick and nobody seemed to pay any attention to the fact that Pam was obviously in a bad mood. I knew she was brooding!

Parvez parked right up on the pavement, but it was almost 3 am so it was OK. His sister was sitting next to me, so I had to move to let her out of the car, and so did Pamela.

valerio viccei

She held the door open for me, but knowing about the few drinks she had had warned me to hold it myself just in case she was tempted to crown me. As soon as I was standing close to her she murmured a low, almost imperceptible 'Bastard' in my ear. I was not too shocked, just worried that the other two might hear and misinterpret it, thinking I had done something awful to the cow. I smiled and did nothing for Parvez's sake. Nobody had heard what she said apart from me. The four of us were now out of the car and the sister proposed that we go upstairs for a drink. When I was certain that the other two couldn't hear me, I looked at Pam and said in a whisper:

'I thought that I had got rid of you for the night, you bitch!'

Chuckling with satisfaction I moved quickly out of range, looking with delight at her enraged expression. Unfortunately, my satisfaction was very brief and was terminated by a full packet of Marlboro which hit me straight in the nuts at ultrasonic speed. I tried to keep the ensuing pain and nausea under control, but there was nothing I could do, but slowly bend down and sit on my heels for a while.

Parvez and his sister were shocked and kept asking how I was feeling — what a dumb question!

The silly cow apologised too and even tried to help me get up, an extremely dangerous thing to do as the temptation to chin her was very hard to resist. However, I kept my temper and said it was nothing. Parvez just muttered a few words of apology on her behalf and that

too fast to live

was that. I thought he must live in another world!

We didn't spend too long in the flat and about an hour later I was in the little Renault again, being driven back to Whites. This time Pam was driving.

She parked outside the hotel and Parvez got out of the car to escort me inside the lobby. It was so late that we would have to wake up the night porter. Pam stayed in the car. I didn't like the way she had been driving the little Renault. She had had far too many drinks!

I told Parvez exactly what I thought but he just shrugged his narrow shoulders as if to say that it would be pointless to ask her to quit driving. I told him that I was going to talk to her about it.

He wished me good luck with a silly grin on his face. I smiled at Pam and slowly put my head inside the little car, whose engine was still running. I thanked her for the lovely evening and for having attempted to make a eunuch out of me. She laughed and said that it was an accident, but anyway I had provoked her! I didn't want to pursue the matter any further, so I admitted that she was right. She looked straight in my eyes and smiled. I was glad Parvez could not see what was going on — for a second I thought the crazy bitch might even kiss me. We were so close. Then I told her, with extreme tact, that it would be safer to call a taxi and leave the Renault in the hotel parking area. For a second or two I thought she might even agree with what I had said as she showed no reaction, but suddenly, slowly and clearly she said, 'Bastard.'

I had had enough of her arrogant behaviour.

valerio viccei

Checking that Parvez was still out of earshot, I whispered in my best English, 'Maybe I am, darling, but you are a bitch, and I know that you are looking for . . .' I couldn't finish the sentence because the crazy girl immediately put the car in gear and drove off with a screech of tyres. Parvez was speechless and I had to call a taxi for him. If I had not moved fast when I did, my head might have rolled on the ground.

*   *   *

Apart from the few occasions I have mentioned, my social life was non-existent. I met with various girlfriends only very late in the evening, in time for a quick dinner in a nice restaurant. I saw David whenever I could and, at the weekends, I sometimes met with Steve and some of my old friends, but that's all.

I tried to rent a flat near the Safe Deposit Centre and I also checked the various hotels nearby, but I couldn't find anything suitable for my needs. I therefore stayed at Whites or, alternatively, at the Kensington Close Hotel. The latter had a safety box facility (how ironic!) while all Whites' rooms had a little safe hidden inside the wardrobe. I made a habit of locking things away whenever I went out. By now, I had eliminated some of my initial options and added a few more frames to the sequence. I knew exactly how many people I needed and where and how to strike. I had also elaborated on a subtle plan to bypass the biggest problem of all: shutting down the premises for a couple of hours and getting away with

too fast to live

it! I knew that the Centre was open seven days a week, and that, apart from Sunday, the box holders could have access to the vaults from 9 am up to 8 pm. They did not need to give any notice and, most of the time, they were totally unpredictable. Everything else was like a Swiss watch, regular and very reliable. Sure, I could easily take them hostage as they came in, but for how long could I hold them? And how would I know if a chauffeur, a relative, or a friend was waiting for them outside?

We were talking hours here, not minutes as for a silly bank in Mayfair. On the other hand, if I shut down the entire place when it was supposed to be open to the public, would it not seem highly suspicious?

I saw my general plan as a chronological sequence of interconnected steps which must be strictly observed. A simple delay in their execution, let alone a mistake, would compromise the entire operation and probably lead to my arrest. This is how I saw it at that stage: an accomplice and I would pose as two customers-to-be. We would call Parvez at a prearranged time and check if everything was fine. He would let us in from the back entrance and escort us directly to the vaults. In so doing we would bypass Fitzpatrick who was always on duty at the front door and knew me well. Once we were down in the strong room, the following steps would be implemented.

1. Neutralise the security guard sitting inside the bullet-proof control room in the basement.
2. Reach the ground floor and, before he could hit

valerio viccei

the silent panic-button, neutralise Fitzpatrick who would be sitting in front of the main entrance.

3. Secure the entire centre.

4. Contact my own security guard by radio and instruct him to come in and close the wooden door of the main entrance.

5. In the same way, contact my other two men and, by a coded message, instruct them to come in through the back door. They would carry two large suitcases containing various tools and all the other equipment apart from the firearms, handcuffs and a chain.

6. Evaluate the quickest way to break the boxes open. Two options would be considered: sledge hammer, or cutting the locks with diamond-coated discs.

7. Make the crucial decision and execute it: everyone would know his individual task and, in turn, all of us would check the monitors connected to the outside video cameras.

8. At a prearranged time; two men would move the plastic sacks with the cash and the more valuable items upstairs, next to the back entrance. On completion of this operation, everybody would stop working. All the tools, the other containers and the remaining sacks would be collected and lined up upstairs, together with the rest of the loot.

9. One of my men, wearing a white overall, would go out through the back door and fetch a removal van parked nearby. He would park it directly in front of the back entrance.

10. Transfer all the stuff piled next to the door into

too fast to live

the van.

11. I would drive the van away with all my team inside and drop them off at a prearranged spot.

12. I would head for the safe house on my own.

This, of course, was the plan in general terms and many of its details had to be reassessed; I didn't have a safe house yet; I hadn't bought the van; I hadn't even chosen the team. But this was all relative. London had plenty of houses for rent, plenty of vans for sale and the world is full of people who want to make money!

The main problem still lay with the two hours I needed to have inside the Safe Deposit Centre.

I took a long time to come up with a feasible solution. I considered many alternatives and I also tried to think as a customer instead of as a robber. I kept asking myself an endless number of questions:

What would make me extremely suspicious?

What would make me feel uneasy?

What would annoy me?

What would be an acceptable justification?

One single customer who got suspicious and we would all be trapped like helpless rats! This was the key problem and I had to be careful, very careful indeed about the way I was going to deal with it.

Another key problem was the recruitment of the four-man team. I could go for professionals but, as I have already pointed out, this is like a double-edged sword. I couldn't take the risk of having the police on my back even before I carried out the operation. I could also try a firm of Israelis or Italians, but this would imply a lot of logistical work and assistance, let alone the risk of immediate identification as far as the nationality of the team was concerned. I also had to consider communication problems and self-sufficiency in case things went wrong; I couldn't provide support for everybody.

I had an idea, a crazy one as usual, but it had worked in the past and I couldn't see why it shouldn't be successful with an operation of such magnitude.

Success lay with planning. If I did it correctly, professionals could well be replaced by amateurs. The idea was still in its infancy and if I could convince myself that it would work, well, I wouldn't need anybody's approval.

In less than a week I had made my mind up and decided that I would try to pull off the biggest robbery in criminal history with a bunch of ordinary people who had never used a gun before, and had never even committed a serious offence. At least I knew they would trust me.

I had a list of names in my mind, and would check their availability. It was my intention not to tell anyone about the nature of the operation until the last minute, nor did I want to give away too many details. This made my task even harder as the trust they needed to place in me must be total, and no hardened criminal would ever agree to that. It was a gamble, a big one, but I was prepared to take it!

Most important of all, I needed one individual who was totally clean and reliable. Someone who would never

too fast to live

be suspected of anything by the police and whose connections could be exploited for logistical purposes. I thought I had him already! As for the team who would assist me physically during the robbery, one of them must be 100% reliable and had to have some balls. I thought I had him already too as I hadn't forgotten how courgeously he had behaved during the drama in the Cavendish Square branch of Coutts Bank.

Peter would have his part to play as well, but what about David and Pinkas? I also had to consider the fitness aspect of these people as there was some heavy physical work to carry out and, apart from Peter, the others were not fit enough. I needed some muscles on the team as well.

CHAPTER 7

The Eternal Triangle

It was quite early in the morning when I phoned Parvez. I needed a piece of information regarding the safety box locks and, as it was my intention to make a final list of the various tools I might need to work on them, I wanted to catch him before he left for the Centre.

'Hello! This is Pam.'

'Hi, Pam. It's me, Gigi, may I speak to Parvez please?'

'I'm afraid you have just missed him, Gigi. He left a few minutes ago.'

'Is he going straight to the Centre?'

'You are in a hurry, aren't you?'

'Well, you know if I don't catch him before he starts his rounds, I won't be able to do it until late afternoon.'

valerio viccei

'Honestly I don't know, but if there is anything I can do for you.'

'Do you feel all right, Pam?'

'Sure, why do you ask?'

'Well, this is the first time you have been nice to me and I wondered . . .'

'Come on now, I am not that bad to you, am I?'

'Hmm, I think you are up to something.'

'Look, Gigi, in a couple of hours I shall be shopping in the West End; if you are not too busy we could have a coffee together. Is that fine with you?'

'Are you serious or are you up to your usual tricks?'

She laughed. 'Right, Gigi, I shall see you at 11.30 in New Bond Street.'

'How about outside Rolex?'

'That's fine.'

'See you there then. Bye bye,' is all I managed to mutter before replacing the phone.

I immediately knew that this game could be very dangerous for the project I had in mind.

She was dressed to kill as she waited outside the main entrance of The Watches of Switzerland, wearing very dark sunglasses and with her long, blond hair resting on her shoulders. Her suit was a very light tone of beige and the brown silk stockings, which I was sure were connected to very naughty suspenders, were a perfect match. The skirt of her suit was tight, as was the jacket and both emphasised her tall, elegant figure. The handbag and shoes had the familiar logo of Chanel. No man in New Bond Street could help noticing her.

too fast to live

I asked the cab driver to stop the car and, amid his protests and as most foreigners do, I got out of the wrong side. An oncoming Porsche almost ran me over and the situation was becoming a little embarrassing, but I did not give a damn and told both of them to get lost. Pam laughed and shook her head as if in disbelief. 'You have a gift for passing unnoticed, Gigi, haven't you?'

'Yeah, you could say that,' I replied, still looking at the mess I had just left behind.

I found it difficult to start a conversation. Pam was smiling and seemed for once to be at ease. It was almost as if we had been best friends or lovers for ages.

'You look stunning, Pam.'

'Well, it is a lovely day and I have the feeling that unless you decide to be run over by a car again, I will have good company for a while.'

'All right, I shall try my best to stick with British traffic rules and I promise that I am going to be good company. By the way, any specific plan?'

'Hmmm, I need to buy some little bits and pieces in a couple of shops in Sloane Street and want to have a look at some shop windows around here. What about you?'

'Nothing specific, so you be leader and I will follow. Just two conditions; we have a proper Italian cappuccino right now and, later on, something to eat together. Is it a deal?'

'Yes, Sir!' she said aping a soldier's salute.

Not surprisingly, I was at a loss for words.

valerio viccei

It was my opinion that Pam was not particularly bright. I don't mean she was stupid, although I did not see her as a shrewd, executive-type woman, but I told myself that I must be careful nevertheless. She was beautiful and very desirable, her command of the language was very good, while mine was still messy and far from sufficient to let me express myself the way I would like to.

We finished her shopping rounds and I was convinced that they were not prearranged at all. It was as though she had been looking for a smart way of passing a couple of hours together, without talking to each other too much and then only about silly things. Just a preliminary meeting before the real business was dealt with.

'It is a little late, Pam, and we haven't booked anywhere for lunch; do you mind if we go to Whites? We already had dinner there with Parvez and you liked it. Also it is one of the very few places where you can drink Krug at the right temperature. What do you say?'

'Anything for a glass of Krug.'

It was June and pretty hot by English standards, but the air conditioning in Whites is perfect as are most of its facilities. We were sitting at a very quiet table in the ground floor restaurant. We went attentively through the very sophisticated menu which, as in every other restaurant in the world, seemed to have been written to confuse the customer. Thank God, most of the staff were Italian and in the end we managed to choose exactly what we wanted: smoked salmon plus caviare to

too fast to live

start, and lobster with some specially prepared sauce as main course.

I opened the hostilities with a simple, 'So, it is about time you tell me what you are up to. Shoot . . .' but this didn't do the trick. She just looked at me in a very provocative way, and replied that she did not understand what I meant.

'Look, we are both grown up and these games can easily get out of hand. I wonder if Parvez would consider what we are doing to be correct.'

'Do you care?'

'Yes, to be honest I do.'

'Right, so what are we doing here?' she said, interrupting me!

'Wait a minute, Pam . . .'

'Oh, come on, Gigi, be honest with yourself!'

'Look, Pam, I am a young man who has no financial problems and loves women beyond belief. You are a very beautiful woman. I am attracted to you and I would do almost anything to get you into bed, but this would be wrong . . .'

'Talking about Helle?'

'Nah . . . forget Helle! Our relationship is very open. She assumes that I screw around at every opportunity, but I feel as though I am betraying Parvez's trust, that's all.'

'Do you really screw around at every opportunity, Gigi?'

'Come on, it is just an expression. You know.'

'Oh, sure, but one that could be very appropriate.'

valerio viccei

'Look, are you just curious or what?'

At least, this managed to make her laugh.

'Gigi, are you still staying here? At Whites, I mean.'

'Yeah, it is a bit expensive but I love this place and I am too fussy to rent a flat. Besides I'm always on the move for one reason or another, so it suits me fine.'

'What sort of clients do they normally have?'

'Well, they are a very exclusive lot, generally speaking. Mainly executives, diplomats, foreign dignitaries and a few tourists. I have seldom met anyone under the age of fifty.'

'Not your favourite hunting ground then.'

'Oh, will you stop it, Pam?'

The conversation continued for a while, but I felt that she was trying to avoid my most direct questions and somehow I was relieved at this, instead of being disappointed. She was a better opponent than I had thought in the first place, therefore I wanted to find out as much as I could about her and yet give very little of myself away. Once coffee was served, however, she dropped her bombshell in a very subtle way.

'How many rooms do they have?'

'About forty, I think.'

'Any outstanding suites?'

'Well, they have just three or four. The one I like most is the Japanese one. They are named after the countries where the style of the furniture comes from. This one is almost entirely black.'

'Are you staying in one of them?'

'Oh no, I have my usual room, the one I like most. I

too fast to live

call it the Hyde Park suite.'

'I see. Do you think that they would let me have a look at the Japanese?'

'Of course they would, provided it is not occupied already.'

'Right, let's ask then.'

We walked together towards the lobby and Giorgio, the head porter, smiled, showing all thirty-two teeth. Knowing me, he already had my room key in his hand as well as a couple of messages. I tried to be as natural as I could and slipped everything into my pocket, trying not to embarrass Pam.

'Giorgio?'

'Yes, Mr Raiman.'

'My lady friend would like to have a look at the Japanese suite. Is that possible?' Unseen by Pam, I shook my head and winked at him. He quickly told me the suite was occupied.

'That's OK, don't worry. Instead, I shall show her the room with the best view of all. I mean the exclusive Hyde Park suite,' I said, walking to the lift and followed by Pam who had not stopped smirking for a single second.

We were in my room. Despite the air conditioning, I opened the French window; the view of Hyde Park almost reaching the balcony was something I wanted to show her. I was really only trying to gain a little extra time before the inevitable happened.

I turned round. There she was sitting on the large, immaculate bed, taking her shoes off and exposing her

valerio viccei

legs all the way up to the naughty suspenders I had so rightly guessed about!

I stared at the ceiling, trying to hide my growing excitement, but my erection was already evident. Her smile told it all.

'Look, Pam. This is becoming highly embarrassing. You'd better stop this or I might do something silly which we might both regret.'

'Who said that I would mind . . .?'

'Christ! Here you are, a most beautiful lady, sitting on my bed with your shoes off and showing half a mile of leg. What do you expect?'

'I would expect you to get some champagne out of the fridge to start with. Then we can talk.'

I did as I was told. When I turned round again, she was sitting on the bed with her legs crossed, Red-Indian style.

'Hmmm, this room looks really nice, Gigi. Considering the way your friend Giorgio downstairs had the key at the ready, you must have had plenty of female visitors lately.'

'Quite a few, actually, but none like you. Believe me.'

'Shall I take that as a compliment . . . or what?'

'Come on, Pam, this is unfair. Were it not because of Parvez, I would already have taken off your clothes and mine!'

'Oh, ho. Are you trying to tell me that you feel some form of obligation towards him?'

'Of course I do, Pam! Can you think of any other

too fast to live

reason why I am not having sex with you right now?'

'I am sorry. I did not think that someone like you would have such high moral standards, Gigi!'

She placed the glass on the night table and was struggling with her shoes, clearly displaying some disappointment.

'Your friend Giorgio will be quite surprised to see me downstairs so early, won't he?'

'Look, Pam. Just sit down and let's talk for a second, OK? I do like you but you are the girlfriend of a good friend of mine. Do you understand that? I feel that our friendship is mutual and this prevents me from having the time of my life with you.'

'It is your choice, Gigi, but let me make it clear that he is not my boyfriend and I am not his girlfriend. Do you get it? I have been pointing it out to you since the very first time we met, if you remember.'

'Wait a minute. I thought you were just being nasty to him for one reason or another.'

'No way, I even pointed out to you that I had my own bedroom in the house.

'Pam, we have met before, haven't we?'

'Sure, Gigi, and thank you for not saying anything. He was a very good friend of Parvez, you see!'

Now I remembered.

'The Italian restaurant in St John's Wood, and that chap with the Bentley . . .'

'Yes, you are right. The other time was when you gave up your seat for me in the coffee shop, but you were probably too busy chatting up that lovely German

173

lady to remember it. Am I right?'

'Well, I didn't say anything because it was none of my business,' I lied.

'How is your Ferrari, by the way?'

The sledgehammer had struck; I knew it was coming. I knew all along and I had been fooling myself. What was I going to do now?

'Ferrari? What Ferrari are you talking about, Pam?'

'The one towed away by the police just opposite our Centre in St John's Wood, Gigi. Look, I know who you are and I even know what you are up to at the Knightsbridge Centre. He tells me everything, my fine Italian friend. He is a selfish wimp and a liar.'

She was not angry, nor was she particularly upset, just disappointed. Her shoes were back on now and she smoothed her skirt while getting up from the bed. I moved much closer to her and at the same time she looked up. Our eyes met and we both smiled.

'Take your shoes off again, Pam,' I said while I gently prevented her from getting up. 'We have plenty of time.'

She let me take charge completely. Very soon we were both undressed. Well, I had taken everything off, while she was still wearing a tiny bra, tinier pants, stockings and suspenders. I decided that I was going to think of her body as a long-awaited Christmas present and unwrap it with infinite patience. I didn't feel guilty any more, not after what she had told me about Parvez.

She was a big girl and her body was even better than I had thought. She looked at my throbbing erection

too fast to live

with a sly smile and giggled like a naughty little girl. To my amazement, she asked jokingly, 'By the way, where do you think you are going to put that thing?'

I gently turned her round and made sure that she understood what I had in mind. As soon as she was on all fours, I positioned myself behind her. I started kissing her loins very slowly and, at the same time, I parted her thighs a little more than she had herself. I struggled for a while with the clasp of her low-cut bra: as soon as I managed to tug it open, her big bouncy boobs spilled free into my waiting hands.

Her full, round bottom was up in the air and the tiny pants already showed a little dampness in the middle. Her nipples were stiff; I squeezed them gently and she gasped with delight.

I started to use my tongue on her lovely, scented body and, at the same time, I gently removed her pants. I petted her slowly, but when her groans indicated that she was already close to climax, I stopped. She was about to protest, but I slightly parted her wet lips with one of my fingers. She was a big girl, but a very tight one indeed. Her body was trembling. I did not penetrate her straight-away, but pressed the tip of my cock against her damp slit. I held it there for a few seconds and played with her clit. Soon I needed all my strength to prevent her from spoiling my game, as she pushed her body backwards with justified madness. I let it coil like a powerful spring and only then did I let it go. She screamed with ecstasy and maybe with a little pain, unprepared for the marathon she was about to endure and the mind-blowing orgasms that would shake her from head to toe. After a couple of hours she was an exhausted and sweat-drenched wreck. As the Chinese say, revenge is a dish best eaten cold.

The few hours of wild sex prevented me from being devastated by the shocking news she had delivered to me with such disarming frankness. Now that her game was up and her cards were on the table, I felt more relaxed and in a position to judge her with total detachment. But what was she after?

If it was her intention to inform on me and Parvez, she would have done so long ago. She must want to make some kind of deal.

We were resting in bed while pleasant music played on the radio. The window was still open and the noise from the traffic was getting worse: until now I had managed to ignore it. I got up and headed for the little refrigerator with the intention of grabbing a bottle of cold Carlsberg.

'Pam, I think we ought to talk for a while. I am sure we can manage to iron things out. Come on, turn round!'

'Ooooh, we're all business now, aren't we?'

'I can't see why we should keep deceiving each other. You are after something and I feel that I have very little choice but to listen to your proposal and, most probably, accept it.'

'Try to understand, Gigi: I am in the middle and I might get into a lot of trouble just because that idiot is letting himself become involved in something as crazy as cleaning out the Centre. To me it all sounded like kids' play, but now it seems that you are deadly serious about it. I don't know what to think any more and I'm a little scared.'

'Right, I am going to be honest with you. I want you to understand that this is not kids' stuff at all, Pam. I appreciate that your position is very difficult and I consider myself very lucky, as you could have informed on both of us already.'

'I hope I did the right thing and that I won't regret it, but I do not want to be involved in it in any way, please,' she begged.

'Fair enough, Pam. But what's your position then, and why did you let me know that you knew what I am up to with Parvez?'

'I don't trust him, and I fear that this business of yours will leave me penniless and in plenty of trouble.'

'Did he promise you some money?'

'Yes, but it has nothing to do with this thing. We agreed, some time ago, that the house we are living in would be sold and the money split between the two of us. But what will happen if he is arrested or if he doesn't keep his word?'

'Well, I understand that things don't look too rosy to you, but what has it to do with me?'

'I trust you.'

'I'm flattered, Pam, but I still don't understand what you are after.'

'Look, if you tell me that you will make sure he keeps his word whatever happens, it's good enough for me and I won't interfere with your crazy schemes.'

'Well, this is no problem at all, but it is a tricky business and I am in no position to tell him that I found out about you.'

'Why, what's the problem?'

'His relationship with me would never be the same again. He would be scared to death. He might think I am going to leave him out in the cold, or even worse. It's a risk I cannot take at this point; I should probably call the whole thing off but it would be too painful, not to mention extremely costly. Please don't tell him anything.'

'If you say so.'

'Look, how much is that house worth?'

'He said that we could make £200,000'

'Right, you have my word that you will get that money, one way or another.'

'Do you mean £100,000?'

'No, I mean all of it. He is such a stupid ass that he deserves to be punished for what he did and for having put you in such a dangerous position. He also lied to me, don't forget. Were I a different character, you could have ended up dead, darling. Do you realise that?'

'Oh, please, Gigi!'

'All right, don't even think about it, but it was a possibility that he should have considered. This is a dangerous business.'

'So what are you going to do about it, Gigi?'

'Leave it with me and you will be all right, I promise.'

too fast to live

'Will you tell him?'

'Only at the right time and after the job is done.'

'What am I supposed to do in the meantime? I don't want to get involved, I am scared.'

'You just listen to me and follow my instructions. I like you and I hope we will continue to see each other when we can. I'll let you know what to do.'

She smiled, kissing me softly on the lips and I couldn't resist the sight of her boobs lifting slightly against my chest.

CHAPTER 8

The Final Stage

Needless to say, the forced agreement I had to make with Pamela was unsettling and very worrying, but I had no alternative. This operation had already cost me too much money, time and sanity. I was prepared to take the risk that she might tell everything to Parvez; the possibility of her contacting the police was far more remote. We met on a very regular basis, spending long evenings in bed together. Sometimes, she even managed to stay until the next morning. She was now an entirely different person: nice, considerate and very eager to please. I returned her kindness by treating her as a lady. I took her out for dinner and lunch, presented her with flowers and little gifts from time to time. I enjoyed her company and I was becoming very fond of her. We were not in love, but you could say that we had become perfect lovers. I felt at ease with her.

Obviously, this new and unexpected turn added to my already complex planning. I had to make sure that Pamela wouldn't create any serious problem after the operation was carried out. I told her to organise a holiday somewhere in Europe. When I said so, she must leave the country and not come back until the dust had settled.

I had decided that the robbery would be carried out on a Sunday afternoon, to be precise on Sunday 12 July. This was a date chosen as the result of repeated, careful checks carried out at the Centre over a period of almost two months. I had spent endless days in the back of a rental van with specially adapted glasses and armed with video recording equipment and a laptop computer. I left a very sensitive voice-activated tape recorder inside my own safety box, and even walked around the area dressed as a silly tourist in shorts and sandals. I did all I could to eliminate the avoidable risks and to find the most suitable time of the day to strike. Apart from this there was the information I had received from Parvez himself.

All the data I had collected was now in front of me in the form of a computer printout and a stack of neat handwritten notes, but no computer could substitute for my brain: machines cannot evaluate the human factor and its unpredictability. The final decisions would be mine and I was well aware of their irreversibility once made. On the other hand, I knew the exact number of people making use of the vaults each day for the last

too fast to live

three months because Parvez had provided me with photocopies of the clients' movement logbook. Through these I had learned how regular the customers were and even at what times they used the premises with most frequency. The logbook also told me how long they spent inside the Centre and if they came on their own. Weekdays, from my point of view, were clearly the worst and after a while I focused my attention decisively on Saturdays and Sundays. In the end, my calculations told me that during Sunday afternoons, between 3 and 5.30 only an average of 3.5 people visited the Knightsbridge Safe Deposit Centre. I concluded that the risk was well worth taking.

I also had to consider that during working weekdays the Centre was open until 8.30 pm, while on Sundays closing time varied between 5.30 and 6.00. Another advantage was the fact that the security firm in charge of setting the alarms and shutting the vault's massive door, usually sent a car with a two-guard crew, while on Sundays it was just one man. He was the so-called 'supervisor', the one who came early in the morning to disconnect the alarms and the various combination locks. He then came once again in the evening to reverse this procedure. This man came in through the back entrance, normally after he had parked his firm's car a few yards away from the door. He rang the bell and, once his colleague in the control room had checked his identity through the camera hidden in the intercom, he was let into the premises. Parvez had not been able to find out if he carried a personal radio-alarm transmitter which sent a silent signal direct to the firm's headquarters, therefore I had to make sure I neutralised him with the utmost firmness as soon as I let him in.

I didn't see any problem at all in doing this, but if the other security guard should be sitting in his car at the same time, I would find myself in the position of having to leave the Centre and hold him at gunpoint while the rest of my team transferred the loot to the van. This was Knightsbridge and such a move would hardly pass unnoticed. It had to be done on a Sunday afternoon.

Besides, having a van parked on any other day in this area without getting clamped would be a miracle!

One more thing in favour of Sunday was the fact that the only staff working at the Centre would be Parvez and the two security guards. The possibility of bumping into new, potential clients was not very good. The getaway route would also be extremely quick and totally traffic-free, while police activity at every level would be almost non-existent.

It was now the end of June and I had contacted the various people I thought might be interested in my proposal. I was not prepared to give any details away and I made it absolutely clear to Peter that none of them should have the slightest idea of the target.

What I had told them was very vague, but they all knew what kind of business I was in and they also knew that in London alone I had already successfully carried out at least four bank raids. I had mentioned that the operation would be much more complex than an ordinary bank robbery, but that the amount of money involved would also be staggering. As I had intimated to Parvez a long time before, I had set out my conditions and made it clear that I would be the only one left in charge of the loot during the time it would take to dispose of it.

They would all leave the country immediately and would get their share as soon as the storm was over. One third of the cash obtained from the job would be divided among the five of them, one third would go to the inside man (whom they did not know as yet, apart from Peter, of course) and one third would go to me.

I explained that, out of my quota, I would have to pay the man who would help me find the bases and the garage, open accounts, get rid of the tools and rubbish and mind me for the first week or so. Furthermore, he would wait for me at a prearranged spot so that I could transfer the loot from the van into huge trunks. Other expenses which I would take care of included various commissions to dealers and middlemen, plus their tickets and accommodation all over the world during the selling phase. All of this would happen while they were resting somewhere in the sun. Nobody disagreed.

I had found the target and I organised the whole thing. I had also put up the necessary money for the operation, paid a large sum of cash to our 'inside man' already and provided the weapons. This alone would entitle me to my share. I would also lead the team and do most of the work myself and I would be left to deal with the disposal phase on my own. Nobody could doubt that I was going to earn every single penny I was

valerio viccei

asking for.

After a meeting or two, however, I realised that I would have to drop one of the guys out. Pinkas was only a mediocre conman. I had offered him the easiest of all tasks and, this notwithstanding, the man didn't stop asking questions and worrying as though he had to take on a whole police station.

I told him that all he would have to do consisted of sitting at the wheel of a white van parked a few hundred yards away from the target. He would be dressed as a security guard but would carry no weapons. His only piece of equipment would be a sophisticated walkie-talkie, via which he would be in contact with me. Not until the whole operation had been successfully carried out, would he be required to drive the van to the back entrance of our target.

I had changed my initial plan in order to avoid any possible suspicion by bystanders and to make it look like an ordinary operation carried out by a security firm. But I had bad vibes about Pinkas now and I suspected that he wouldn't be able to stand the pressure of sitting inside the van on his own for almost two hours without panicking. If he panicked, he would grab his radio to try to convince me that something was wrong on the outside and that he had to leave. This would mean aborting the operation. I decided to drop him.

Unfortunately I had left to him the task of purchasing a white van and fitting it out in a way that would make it resemble a proper security vehicle. He had also to find two full uniforms and have the

too fast to live

'NOTICE TO ALL CUSTOMERS' labels professionally printed.

The 12th was just ten days away and Pinkas had still done nothing. I would have to go and get the van with him, not to mention kick his ass in order to obtain the labels from a friend of his. I told him nothing about my idea of dropping him out; I would contact him after the robbery and give him the task of acting as middleman with the gold and diamond dealers.

Another problem I was facing was the security guard on duty in the control room on 12 July. I couldn't wear any mask, of course, as I had to act as a potential customer, but this particular guard knew that I was already a customer and a personal friend of the owner as well. This would make him feel more relaxed and ready to show me the security arrangements but, on the other hand, Parvez would then have to admit that he knew me and claim that he had been the victim of a carefully planned deception over the course of a few months. With Pamela in between us this was a very alarming prospect. She would certainly be interviewed as soon as possible, and her holiday in Spain couldn't last for ever.

I had to convince Parvez to get rid of that particular guard with some excuse and have him replaced by a new chap who had never seen me before. This was swiftly done; from Saturday 11 July a new guard would be on duty in the control room.

As my factotum, I had chosen Steve Mann. He was a Jewish guy in his thirties with plenty of good connections in the business world. He was not a criminal at all, but worked for Abbey Life, which made him an unlikely object of police suspicion after a robbery of such magnitude. Our common bond was cocaine. Although he did not know my real name, let alone that I was a wanted man, he had repeatedly told me that if I ever needed some help in my 'business', he would be available. He needed money, he kept saying, and also felt some sort of moral obligation towards me because of the hospitality and the cocaine he had repeatedly received from me on social occasions. He obviously thought that I was some kind of drug dealer connected to the Italian underworld and, for the time being, this suited me fine. I told him that his co-operation might be useful in the near future and that, as proof of his commitment, he should do a couple of errands for me. I needed to rent a small house with a garage in the North London area. If this proved to be impossible, I would settle for a large flat in a very discreet block with a concealed driveway. I had no references, I was not prepared to offer any and the place would be rented in a phoney name. I would pay cash in advance for six months and go up to £400 per week. As soon as he found a suitable place and the contract was signed, there would be a grand in it for him! The second thing I asked him to find was a set of four VHF hand-held programmable transceivers.

He asked no questions and made no objections. Within forty-eight hours I had the walkie-talkies and, the day after, a choice of at least four houses and three flats to inspect. The man seemed to be very efficient and extremely discreet. I was very satisfied with him and I

too fast to live

thought that I might start to check out his availability a little further. During this same week I popped in at his office at lunch time and invited him to have something to eat at Wolfe's. After a general chat, I asked him if he could spend the afternoon with me and help me to purchase some tools in Selfridges. He said that it was OK with him, but that he knew plenty of shops where tools were much cheaper. I thanked him but pointed out that money was not a problem and that the operation I was setting up would be so profitable that we could afford to buy solid gold tools. I waited for his comment, but he made none.

I was sure he had been thinking about a huge drug deal, and that now the number of different tools I had mentioned must be puzzling him. I decided that it was time to make it clear that I was after some safety deposit boxes. Only then did he ask where that would be. I told him that it would not be appropriate for him to find out where and when, at least not yet, but I wanted to know if this made any difference to him. He said that it did not . . . as long as I knew what I was doing.

The next day Steve came to pick me up at Whites, where I was staying once again. He had with him a list of the various places he had managed to find. Most of them had been obtained through an estate agency where his brother had worked in the past, therefore he had been entrusted with the keys and this sounded terrific to me. I would be in a position to check whatever I wanted without being observed by the attentive eyes of the agency's representative, nor would I be asked questions which I might not be able to answer.

As a matter of fact, most of the little houses were fine, but they had no garage and their driveways were all unprotected. On the day of the robbery I would be observed by unseen neighbours while transferring huge trunks from a vehicle to the house; should my photo appear in the papers or on television, they could easily put two and two together. Our search continued.

A penthouse did not fit the picture I had of my ideal safe house, but I was running out of time and I couldn't afford to ignore any valid alternative. The place we found was in Redington Road, Hampstead.

The entrance to the old house was just perfect, it was completely hidden from view and a little park with huge trees made the whole building almost invisible. It was love at first sight and I did not care if I had to sweat buckets in order to transport the trunks all the way up to the top floor. Apart from this, we discovered that there were only three other flats, one on each floor, and that not all of them were occupied at the moment.

Once we were in the apartment itself, I couldn't hide my happiness: it was huge and, being on the top floor, it had a full view of all the surrounding area. It was fully furnished and had rooms to spare; even the telephone was working. I took it.

The next day, Friday 3 July, I moved in, with Steve helping to carry the various cases and bags. Some of them contained the tools purchased in Selfridges, some the security uniforms and the walkie-talkies, while in a small briefcase there were two weapons, and all my plans

too fast to live

and memos. I surveyed this lot, now neatly arranged on the carpet of the main bedroom, and realised that although a few items were still missing, most of the work had been done and what had been just a crazy idea only two months ago was now becoming reality.

During the last two weeks before the 'day' I kept on meeting with Parvez almost on a daily basis. There was a lot to do. I could rely on the others a little, but this did not mean that I was prepared to overlook even the smallest detail. Everything would be done by the book.

At one of our final appointments, I asked Parvez to provide me with a safety-box lock of the type that was fitted in the steel door as soon as a customer had chosen their box size. I assumed that taking this apart would give me a chance of understanding the way it worked and to discover if, by any chance, it would be better to attack the lock directly, instead of the steel door itself.

After hours of careful examination, I came to the conclusion that the lock was definitely very secure and that trying to drill through it would take quite a lot of time, even with the powerful electric drills I had bought in Selfridges. I also had to consider the possibility that the boring tools fitted to the drills would snap repeatedly, and that the time necessary for their replacement was a negative factor. On the other hand, there was a flimsy metal spring clip at the bottom of the lock, held in place by a tiny groove in the solid brass cylinder; once this was removed, all the other components could simply be pushed backwards and out of the way.

valerio viccei

With the help of a very heavy vice I started to work on this new idea. In the end I discovered that by hitting the lock right in the middle of the key hole with a specially shaped hammer, I could manage to make the metal ring jump out of its groove and so gain access to its mechanism. At this point, the steel pin preventing the box door from being unlocked could easily be removed with my bare hands.

I also discovered that the lock was joined to the door by a couple of simple bolts; should the metal spring clip stay in its place, there was no way that the bolts' support could withstand the powerful blow of a very heavy sledgehammer. One way or another, the lock would slide backwards and make room for the smaller tools with which I could attack the steel pin.

Having discovered this, I rushed out to buy a sledgehammer and, with a diamond-coated disc fitted to an electric grinding machine, I carefully shaped it. The job was hard and extremely noisy, but in the end I came up with a tool weighing about twenty pounds and with one of its sides resembling the lock's cylinder. I was certain it would work fine. Considering that all of the tools would be brought into the Centre by two of my men inside rigid suitcases, I also had to shorten the massive hammer's handle in order that it would fit inside the larger of the two cases.

By now one long list of items I needed and another of various, unsolved problems were both reduced to just a few entries. Of these, the one worrying me most was the garage. As I said before, although the penthouse

too fast to live

suited my needs perfectly well, there was no garage, and this would create some serious problems. All the stuff taken from the boxes would initially be placed inside strong, green plastic bags. Once filled they measured about five foot in height, by four in diameter. I had tested their resistance to stress and discovered that they wouldn't break even if loaded with a hundred and fifty pounds. I might have been a little too optimistic, but I had bought twelve of them. Add the two suitcases and the two pilot cases that my partner and I would carry when posing as potential customers, and that made a hell of a lot to unload from the van. A very suspicious lot, I might add!

No, I needed a garage in which to transfer all the stuff from the green bags to three huge, but inoffensive-looking trunks. Steve had better come up with a bright idea very soon!

He called me early in the morning and said that we might have an ideal solution: he would come to see me at the Redington Road flat in half an hour. His idea was pretty good, as far as it went, and worth looking into. He told me that most of the tenants of the block where he lived owned a garage, and that there was a row of them just a few yards from the main building itself. Their driveway was protected from view and on a Sunday afternoon nobody would be around. He had also checked with one of the tenants, a very old man who never set foot in his garage, and asked him if he could use it for a few days. The old man had agreed to that, but had pointed out to him that a new lock would have

valerio viccei

to be fitted and that there was some rubbish to be removed. Apart from this, Steve could use it any time he wanted to.

It sounded good to me. Besides, his place was just ten minutes' drive from Redington Road and a very quiet one at that. Once inside the garage, we could unload the van's contents, place them in the trunks, change the van's plates, get rid of it and, finally, go back and move the whole lot to Redington Road in the rented estate car. I was very positive about it!

We went to check the garage together; it was a little messy and the lock was broken but, apart from that, everything else was fine. The door couldn't be seen from the main building, nor from any other nearby block of flats. Steve would fit the lock and tidy it up immediately.

Of course, Pinkas, the gutless jerk, had not even bought the van yet, so I had to go and get one with him as soon as possible. We bought the van the day after the garage lock had been fitted by Steve. I had to settle for a white Renault in very good condition, but this was not a van normally used by security firms and therefore I had to abandon the idea of trying to make it look like one. It would just be an ordinary white van. If some nosey witness was going to think what we were doing with it on the day of the robbery was odd, well, we would make them believe it was an ambulance and we were a paramedical crew. A loaded gun works miracles.

One more little problem was presented by the fact that the van was far bigger than the one I had had in mind and now I wouldn't be able to get inside the

too fast to live

garage with it. This meant that Steve and I would have to take one extra little risk in unloading it just outside the garage door.

Having dropped Pinkas out, only one of the men would now have to wear a security guard uniform and, because of this, I had to reassess this aspect of the plan once again. I simply reverted to my original idea. One of the team would go out of the back entrance of the Centre as soon as I had neutralised the supervisor and he would then park the van right outside the door, where we would load it. No problem at all and more money for each of the lads.

Everything seemed to be ready and I couldn't help thinking that I had done a terrific job. My command of the language was still far from perfect and this, plus the fact that I was a man on the run, had greatly handicapped my task, but will power and experience enabled me to overcome the difficulties I had faced all along. I knew very well that this operation would mark my future for ever, one way or another. The fact that I could end up with a bullet in my head or, worse, with a twenty-year prison sentence didn't bother me at all. This prospect was something I had learned to cope with as a youngster. I meant to carry out an armed assault — in full daylight — on a Safety Deposit Centre. This was not simply a robbery and to pretend otherwise would be childish. This was Knightsbridge, with its special place in the world and in the very heart of London.

I was about to violate one of the safest vaults on earth and take all of its security staff hostage for two hours, but

valerio viccei

why was I doing it? Was it just for the money and the luxury that came with it? Well, it would be impossible to deny that this was one of the main factors, but, on the other hand, I had always lived surrounded by luxury and I had always had plenty of money. So, why was I taking such risks against all odds and all reason? I definitely saw it as a challenge — the ultimate one — to society as a whole. If successful, the operation would leave its mark for ever, giving me satisfaction of such significance that I might even consider the possibility of retiring. I would not need to prove anything to myself or anyone ever again.

My motivations were far from being honourable, but I considered them no worse than the motivations that drive most people at the top. They might use their power, their money, their connections; I would use my brain and my gun. I was not going to feel sorry for those manipulators who had hidden millions of pounds in cash or silly decorations in gold and diamonds in their safety deposit boxes.

At this stage the plan was almost complete and only a few details still had to be reassessed in order to match the continuous, unavoidable changes that such a complex operation requires in order to show flexibility.

Two members of my team would come from overseas and they would need logistical support and a safe base. Redington Road was out of the question as, apart from Steve Mann, who had rented it on my behalf, nobody would ever know its whereabouts. Another place was therefore needed, but this was a relatively easy task compared to the rest. Such a base would only be needed for the few days preceding the robbery and nothing suspicious would ever happen there. As a matter of fact, I re-rented the flat in Princess Mews where Helle and I had stayed soon after my escape from St John's Wood. The estate agency staff dealt mainly with tourists and short-term tenants, therefore, when someone enquired if that specific flat was available for a few weeks, they asked no questions.

Once this second safe house was obtained, I proceeded to purchase the estate-car needed to transfer the trunks from Steve's garage to Redington Road. I wasn't looking for a particular make, nor was I interested in a very large station-wagon because I considered that two trips were necessary in any case, thus when, thanks to David, I obtained a Volkswagen Passat in perfect condition, I was entirely satisfied.

As far as I was concerned, everything had been carefully arranged and nothing could stop me from carrying out the robbery.

The reader may wonder why, apart from Stephen Mann, Parvez Latif and, to a certain extent, Peter O'Donohue, I have not mentioned the names of the various individuals who participated in the operation. This is not very easy to do when legal proceedings have yet to be completed and while some people are still maintaining their innocence. All but one, in fact, behaved pathetically, if not shamefully, but this does not entitle me to sink to their level.

To solve this dilemma, I will indicate the men who

valerio viccei

participated in the robbery in the same way I did during my questioning by the police and while giving evidence at the Old Bailey. I will use numbers instead of names. This will not affect the reconstruction of events in the slightest, mainly because these people played a very small part during the robbery and none whatsoever during the planning phase. Even during our radio contacts, we avoided referring to each other by name and used numbers instead.

Our final meeting was in the Kensington Close Hotel's spacious lounge. I chose this place because it was usually extremely busy and its many customers seemed to spend a lot of time there having a chat over a drink. Nobody paid any attention to anybody and that was exactly what I wanted. We were all smartly dressed, apart from Peter, who, with his long hair and colourful outfit, looked more like a pop star than a bank robber. This was fine with me.

Some of the people did not know each other. It was now time to introduce them to one another and to explain what was going on. Having to deal with amateurs, I had to play all my cards very close to my chest. Before I said anything, I asked them once again if they wanted to quit; within five minutes they would no longer have such a choice. They all wanted to stay in.

Different backgrounds, nationalities and mother tongues did not seem to be a problem to our small party. We all communicated in plain English and I tried my best not to confuse anyone. I thought that my crazy idea would work fine; they trusted me completely and

Some you win, some you lose, my cheeky self on visit- Parkhurst.

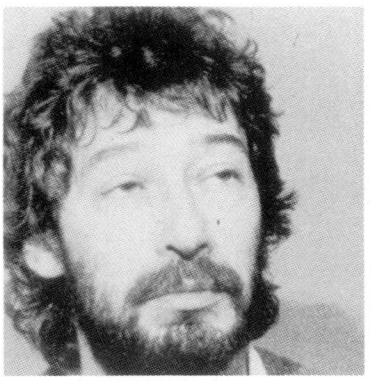

Stephen Mann: The Grass

David Poole

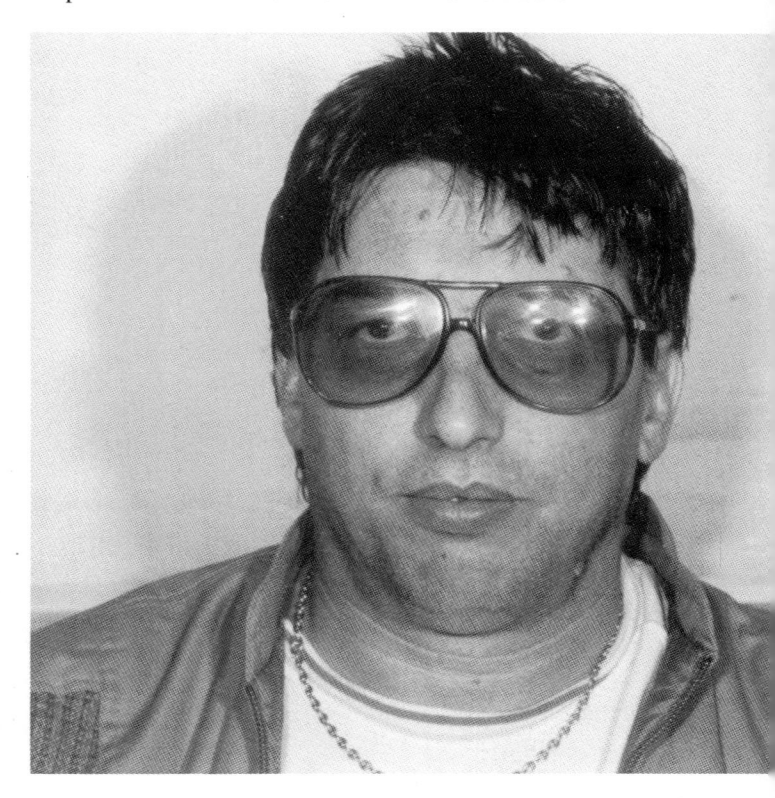

Israel Pinkas

Eric Rubin

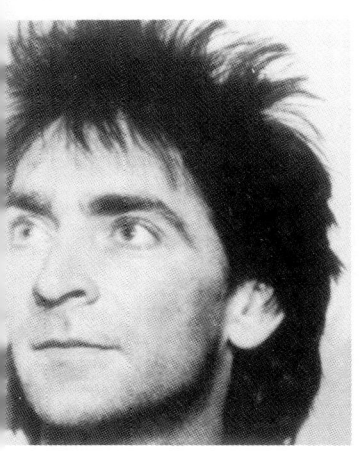

Peter O'Donohue

Parvez Latif

Top: The Knightsbridge Safe Deposit Centre.

Near right: The fake sign taped to the door of the Centre during the raid.

Far right: Scene of devastation. The heart of the Safe Deposit Centre after we had completed the raid.

We apologise to all our Customers for any inconvenience caused to them during the improvements to our Security System

Business as usual from tomorrow

– Thank you

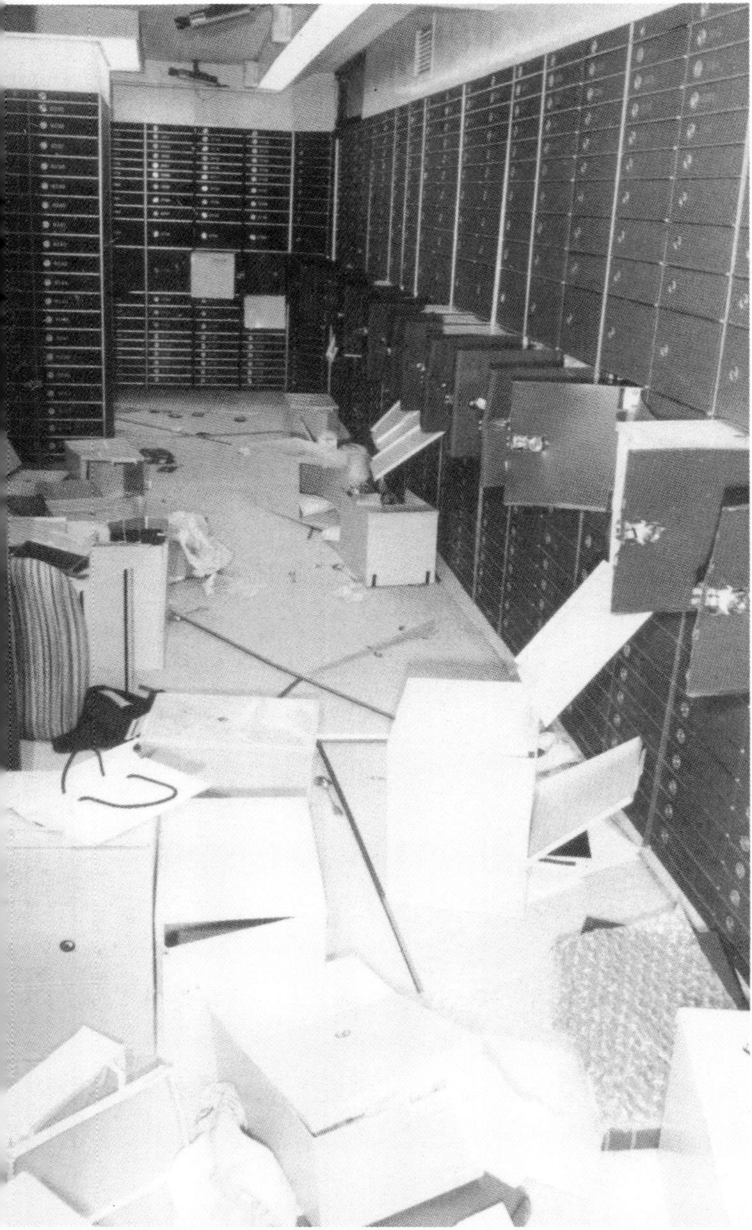

Parkhurst prison high security risk visiting room—
Top: With my good friend Wayne, another wolf.
Above: With Helle.

Top left: Together with my father Ibiza 1986.
Top right: My ex-wife Noemi in a recent photo.
Below: My family celebrating Christmas 1991.

With my father-Parkhurst, 1992

too fast to live

listened very attentively to what I said.

It was my intention to go over the main topics very briefly, just to satisfy their natural curiosity, and let them absorb their new roles. I said that the job was now three days away and that it would be a Safe Deposit Centre in Knightsbridge. Only when I mentioned its whereabouts, just opposite Harrods, did I notice a little concern in their eyes. I explained that the true value of what we would get was obviously impossible to calculate in advance and that everything would depend upon many factors: the key ones being time and synchronisation. The longer we managed to stay inside the premises and the quicker we worked, the more boxes we could break open. I also emphasised that we had a member of the staff on our side and that he would be working there on the day of the robbery. I did not elaborate on this and they asked no questions. Apart from number 2 and myself (1), nobody else would be required to carry a weapon. Myself, number 3 and number 4 would each have a two-way radio. We carried on chatting about the whole thing as if it were the most ordinary event in the world and called it a day only when a table too close to the one we were sitting at was occupied by a couple of Americans.

I spent the evening with my two overseas friends. They knew least about the operation and I thought that they would appreciate having a look at the target itself. Knightsbridge during the rush hour can be pretty frightening to someone who is about to take over a Safety Deposit Centre and I thought that lack of traffic and of tourists milling around would make my friends feel a little more comfortable. Once we reached the Centre, which by then was closed, I simply indicated the front door and said: 'That's it, lads; what do you think then?'

A simultaneous 'Fucking hell!!' was the reply, at which we all laughed non-stop for a couple of minutes. I explained what was going to happen on Sunday and how we would get in through the back entrance which, once it was shown to them, managed to make them feel a bit more comfortable. The more I told them, the more they nodded and I knew I was doing just fine. Needless to say, I considered number 2 and number 4 the most efficient members of my team, therefore I wanted them to absorb as many details of the operation as they could. They asked many questions, of course, and I was glad that the obsessive care which I had paid to the planning now gave me the opportunity to reply with extreme confidence, and without ever disappointing their expectations.

One of the questions was: 'Gigi, what about the odds?'

I did not need time to reflect; I had been calculating them for ages.

'We will get in 100%; I will get the security staff 100%; we will break open at least 80 large-sized boxes 100%; we will leave the premises together with the loot 70%. Will we get away with it? Well, lads, there is no way anybody can calculate that. So let's forget about it and get on with our job!'

too fast to live

I drove them to the flat in Princess Mews and told them that they would spend the remaining days there together and that, apart from me and the two teammates, nobody else knew they were there. In fact, even Steve and Helle, who, incidentally, helped me to rent the flat, did not know that other people were staying there at the time. I also told them that the following day we would meet again and I would show them the various maps and notes, the tools and the walkie-talkies. We would go over each individual task until everything was clear to all of them. I stressed that they should start organising their departure as soon as possible because they would leave the country immediately after the job — actually on the same evening! We would keep in touch via my bleeper, whose number was known to them already. They also had a personal code-name to be used for this specific purpose.

I went back to the penthouse, which wasn't far from the other flat. I was the only one who knew everybody and everything, while the others knew only what they needed to know. I had to make sure that everybody was going to carry out his own task without interfering with those of the others. I also had to see Pamela and Parvez, to make sure that the former would leave the next day, as already agreed, and that the latter did not change his bloody mind at the last minute. One of those two could easily screw everything up, and they would soon be beyond my control.

Once back in my flat, I went through my notes and memos again as though I was reading them for the first time. Nothing can be perfect, of course, but total dedication can bring us very close, and I was satisfied that, operationally, things looked almost perfect. They could not be improved any further.

I sat down at my 'working' desk, surrounded by all sorts of technical equipment, maps, computer printouts, stop-watches and so on. I turned off the main light and used a desk lamp instead. I had something in mind; soon I would need total darkness.

I laid some sheets of drawing paper in front of me and, with a pencil, I drew a long line representing the route from what would be our operational base in Croydon to Brompton Road. From there I drew a second route through Hyde Park and the Finchley Road to Lyttelton Road, Hampstead, where Steve Mann lived. I wrote down numbers and references along the whole route; they indicated the various 'legs' of the operation and their ideal times. Having done this, I switched on a sophisticated tape recorder, turned the desk lamp off and then relaxed in my comfortable chair. The machine was extremely sensitive and I could speak very softly: 'Zero time, leg one. Start.'

The green digits on the recording set slowly, but inexorably, indicated the passing seconds. It would be a long night.

I mentally covered every single move we would be making on the day of the robbery, starting from zero time when we left the operational base, established in number 3's flat. By then everybody would be dressed up, tooled up and briefed again about his assignment. I calculated the time necessary to reach Pont Street where we would stop in order to make a phone call to the Centre. When I imagined parking the Passat just in front of the phone box, I softly said into the mike: 'Leg one completed.'

I then paused to calculate the time necessary to make the call and to reach Trevor Square, where I would finally abandon the car. I would walk towards the Centre, covering the few hundred yards at a very slow pace.

The imaginary sequence was so realistic that I could see the details of the little park, the back door of the Centre, the vaults, the control room . . . everything. I looked at the machine's digital timer; forty minutes had already passed. I continued to insert more frames and the time flew.

The big green bags were filled up, the supvervisor was handcuffed and led to the viewing room. 'Leg seven completed.'

The white Renault van was finally parked outside Steve's garage and then, only then, I said: 'Leg ten completed; mission accomplished!'

I looked again at the clock on the tape recorder; it showed 04.15. I could now transcribe all the data on to my handmade map, have a hot cup of coffee and start all over again. I repeated the operation from scratch, but this time I covered the clock with a sticker. I tried to relive the same scenes, drive along the same route at the same speed, evaluate the same problems and make the same decisions. I must be sure; good timing makes the difference between success and failure. My tiredness did not concern me; I had to carry on. The time was 04.07! Very good!

Tomorrow I would try once again and on Saturday afternoon I would finally drive from our base to Knightsbridge; I would call Parvez at the Centre; I would do everything I would do the following day, apart from walking through the back door.

I wanted things to go smoothly. The secret of a good movie consists of rehearsing the scenes over and over again until the actors know exactly what to say, where to stand or sit, where and how to scratch their heads, without having to think about it. That was exactly what I was trying to achieve.

When I walked through that little back door on Sunday, when I grabbed the security guard by the scruff of his neck and gently aimed my gun at his head, I would feel no excitement at all. I would be doing something I had done repeatedly in my mind: this would be just one more time.

I was only concerned about the others, but because of this I had made sure that I wouldn't need any of them until the most dangerous and tricky steps had been completed. In theory, this meant that they couldn't screw things up. Still, I did need them and I feared that if anyone lost his bottle at the last minute I would be in deep shit and there was nothing I could do about it.

By now the sun was already up and I desperately needed some sleep. In the last two weeks I had slept for an average of four hours a day, and that was a really

too fast to live

dangerous thing to do in my position, but there was still a lot to be done. If there was no time to rest, I would still survive.

*   *   *

Pamela and I were sitting in her little white Renault. She was still a little angry with me because a few days earlier I had missed an appointment with her and she had had to wait for over an hour in a rather dubious part of Queensway, just opposite the hotel where I had a room at the time. People walking around must have thought that she was a high class hooker and her rage was clearly expressed in a message she handed to the hotel's receptionist but which I received only at 5 am the following morning! I was giving her her last instructions and begging the lovely lady to follow them no matter what. I also handed over to her a large amount of cash so that she could stay where she had decided to go for as long as proved necessary. She also had to fly out whenever I told her to, even at very short notice. She had my bleeper number and her code name was Nadia. I told her to call me as soon as she arrived and to leave a number where I could contact her. Sunday was just forty-eight hours away and she would no doubt find out what had happened directly through Parvez.

We kissed tenderly and she wished me luck, looking at me with a mixture of fondness and sadness at the same time. She obviously realised that we might never meet again and that, by Sunday evening, I could be lying on a

valerio viccei

slab in the morgue!

*   *   *

It was Saturday morning. In less than thirty hours I would find out if the last two months of intensive planning had been enough. I had done all I could to prevent blunders, but the unpredictability factor is always the one most feared by people in my line of work and I am no exception.

That afternoon I would proof-test communication, route, vehicles and weapons. I also had to meet Parvez for the last time and speak to Helle. This was going to be a very delicate task because I felt some obligation towards her and, despite all my other girls, I thought the world of her. She knew nothing, of course, and I did not want her to know anything for her own safety and peace of mind, but should things work out the way I had planned, she would be able to put two and two together! I would see her on Sunday morning and tell her that I must leave for a while but that I would also call her during the evening. If I didn't call, something very bad would have happened to me and she should contact my lawyer and my family immediately.

I had a long, hot shower and a huge breakfast. I hadn't slept as much as I should have, but adrenalin was pumping hard through my body and I felt relaxed as usual. In a short while Steve would come and pick me up, so I wanted to enjoy these last few minutes of deep meditation. Nor for a single instant did I think of

too fast to live

quitting, but all of a sudden, I lifted the phone and dialled a familiar number in Italy. I wanted to speak to my mother and tell her how much I loved her. I might not have the opportunity again and I would never forgive myself for that!

* * *

It was the Saturday afternoon test-run. Number 2 was sitting next to me in the Passat and we had just left number 3's flat. My tape recorder was on and I checked a stop-watch at every prearranged spot. The timing was perfect and I was pleased after having spent so many sleepless nights on this.

Number 2 was not a kid any more and his health was poor. I wanted this to be his last exploit, the one after which he could retire to a quiet and comfortable life. Apart from my old man, nobody else would be allowed to smoke in the car, but he was doing exactly that and I did not mind at all!

Peter and number 4 were right behind us in the Renault van, while number 3 was driving his own car. They all seemed very relaxed and this was a good sign. I felt good too!

We stopped just outside the phone box in Pont Street and, as we were in touch via the radios, I told the others to park their vehicles nearby. I got out of my car, slipped inside the phone box and dialled Parvez's personal line at the Centre. As previously agreed, he was quick to reply. The timing was spot on once again!

I told him to meet me outside the pub in Montpelier Place in ten minutes. He sounded as calm as ever.

I instructed my team to stay out of sight for some time. I did not elaborate upon this, but they knew that I was about to see my inside man. I was not yet prepared to let them know who the man was. They accepted this and asked no questions.

Ten minutes later Parvez greeted me with his best smile and we shook hands like two old friends.

Apart from opening his big mouth to Pamela, he had behaved perfectly well until now. I didn't know quite what to make of his behaviour, but I would only have to live with my doubts for a few more hours. We walked along the pavement. The area was as busy as ever and nobody seemed to pay any attention to us.

I told him that everything was fine and that things looked very good. I was therefore in a position to confirm that the following day he would receive my phone call at 15.00 hours, but that one of my men would also have to speak to the security guard a few minutes later. My call would reach him directly on his personal line, while number 3 would use the ordinary line and ask Fitzpatrick about the availability of boxes. I wanted the guard to be mentally prepared for the arrival of a potential customer. Of course the one who dealt with us would be Parvez, but a guard is always a guard and he would want to know what was going on. Once he knew a customer was expected, his curiosity would be satisfied and we would be able to walk down to the vaults almost unobserved.

too fast to live

Parvez said that there should be no problem and that, as some of the customers did exactly that, the guard wouldn't be suspicious at all. I then handed him one of the hand-held radio sets and, having explained how it worked, I suggested that he should hide it under his jacket, turn the volume down and go back to the Centre. I also wanted him to go straight down to the vaults. I would keep talking all the time and he must try to remember in which areas the signal was weaker and if, by any chance, there were areas where it did not receive any signal at all, I would call at his house at midnight and we would have a brief chat about the few details which I still considered not entirely clear. He nodded and left with a big smile. Almost immediately I started speaking into my own set, talking a lot of nonsense numbers, code words and so on. When I was satisfied that he had had enough time to cover the whole Centre, I headed towards my car to think about the next move.

I arrived at Parvez's house after midnight, but took care not to park the Passat in the road where he lived, and so walked for a few hundred yards instead. The night was not cold and the sky was cloudless, but there was not a soul to be seen.

We sat down in the living room and had a drink; he seemed very calm and I wondered whether he fully realised the enormity of what we were about to do.

I asked him to repeat every single move he would have to make from the time of my call onwards. Apart from a few details, he did a very good job. I was satisfied that he wouldn't forget anything.

Just before I left I asked him if he needed any more cash for the next few days as business was not doing well. I couldn't afford to have him bounce a cheque while the police were all over the place: it would look too suspicious. When he said that some cash would be handy, I suggested that the following day he should carry a briefcase with him and leave it in his office. He should place two very large manila envelopes in it, one of which should be addressed to his lawyer and the other to his accountant. I explained that once I had emptied some of the safety deposit boxes, and while he was still chained to a pillar, I would go upstairs and fill both manila envelopes with bundles of new, large-denomination bank notes.

Should things go wrong, or should I need to hide for much longer than I planned to, he would be in a position to use that money for the business. I would also seal the envelopes. If the police happened to chance upon them during their search of the premises, they would never dream of opening two sealed letters addressed to a lawyer and to the firm's own accountant.

The sly son of a bitch smiled and thanked me.

When I was about to leave I asked him where Pamela was and, smiling again, he said: 'I told her to have a break in Spain for a while. She did not want to go, so I had to insist. Everything is fine now, so don't you worry about her.'

I did not like this but had to admit that he was a professional liar. This, I thought, would come in useful during his questioning by the police. I grinned and

too fast to live

shook his hand with unusual energy. I looked straight into his eyes and then told him: 'Parvez, there is no way back now and I want you to know that. If you think of quitting I feel obliged to make it clear that things will turn nasty very quickly for you. Just be aware of that, my friend, and everything will be fine.'

'I understand that, Gigi, but don't worry, I'll go all the way. Now go and get some sleep. You look very tired, and it is already tomorrow . . .'

CHAPTER 9

Like Watching a Movie

Sunday, 12 July — Redington Road, North London

I knew this was going to be the most important day of my life but somehow it didn't seem any different from yesterday. The tape recorder had proved a good ally and I felt as if I had already lived this day over and over again.

I managed to trace Helle very easily as she was staying with some friends in Camden Town. I told her that I would be there in half an hour. I checked my notepad once again and made some more calls. One was direct to Steve. I told him that he must stay at home until 7.00 pm and must not go out for any reason. If everything went smoothly I would be there at 6.00, but I wanted some

valerio viccei

extra time, just in case.

Steve wanted to know what he was supposed to do if I didn't turn up at all. I had not contemplated this so far, but I needed to be realistic and put my unshakeable determination aside for a moment. I told him that, if he had not heard from me by 8.00 pm he must get rid of everything I had left in the penthouse and then get away from London himself for a while. He said that was fine with him and I could feel that my optimism had been highly contagious as he now sounded as if he was no longer thinking that such a thing could happen. He just wished me the best of luck and rang off. It was 10.00 am. In four hours I would start the countdown: four more hours and it would all be over. My confidence was total and nothing was going to stop me!

As if to reaffirm this I took my handgun from the night stand; I slowly checked the clip and then jacked a shell into the chamber. Without a second thought I tucked it in my waistband at the small of my back. I was in business!

As I had known already, talking to Helle was not easy, but she was a good girl and spared me embarrassing questions — questions which would have remained unanswered in any case. I was, and still am, very fond of her. Although the hurt I had endured with Noemi was not over yet, I already thought of Helle as more than simply a girlfriend. She knew my family and had all my trust, but I am in a line of work where you can't afford to be totally open with people. Even becoming too close to them is a risk . . .

too fast to live

I drove Helle around for a while and when I finally dropped her off, at her friends' place, she was an extremely worried lady. She knew that if I didn't call her sometime that night, the worst would have happened and that the TV and newspapers would tell her the whole story.

*   *   *

Croydon, South London — 1300 hours

We were all sitting in the small living room of number 3's flat. The atmosphere was relaxed and each person seemed quite confident with his individual tasks. My final brief was intentionally very sharp and stuck to essentials. I didn't want any of them to get mixed up right now and could only hope they would stick to the instructions already received. Then I noticed that Peter was still wearing his usual 'colourful' outfit and asked him to get changed quickly. His expression told it all: the idiot had forgotten to bring some smart clothes with him, with the result that he would attract more attention than a policeman in full uniform walking across Parkhurst exercise yard. I yelled at him but only a little. I couldn't afford to take risks; all I needed was this fool getting the hump. I carried on.

The equipment was checked one more time, as were the car keys, the padlock, the handcuffs, gloves, balaclavas and so on. When I asked them to go through their pockets once again and make sure they were absolutely empty, some of them gave me a weary glance. I ignored it and thought of my many good friends who were still doing time for just such a stupid oversight.

The minutes passed slowly, with the result that number 3 was growing a little too impatient, while 2 and 4 kept wiping every single item for the umpteenth time. At least it was a positive reaction to the mounting pressure.

The two weapons lay on top of the table and I busied myself with cleaning them. One was my faithful Beretta and the other a sawn-off shotgun. I knew that we really wouldn't need the firearms at all. The way I had planned the operation would enable me to overpower both the guards and their supervisor with my bare hands, but this could lead to pointless reaction on their part which, in turn, would generate a fracas. Surprise was to be the winning factor in this game; if the first guard let out a yell, Fitzpatrick would hit the panic button immediately and all would be lost! I couldn't afford such a thing to happen. The psychological threat of a gun would immediately establish the rules of the game and decide who was going to be in charge. It was the guards who would need me to carry a weapon in order to find an excuse not to react. Very few non-professionals understand these things.

One more thing I had learned during many years in the field was that every armed member of a team had the right to choose the way he would deal with his own weapon. I would have preferred 2 not to load his weapon, but the final decision lay with him; if confronted

too fast to live

by armed people he should, I believed, be in a position to fight them off. Too many times robbers have been killed when they were holding unloaded weapons. If this was to happen to him I would never forgive myself. I looked intently at him but a nod from him confirmed that the old man was not thinking of getting away with a lesser sentence. He could prove to have been a dangerous choice, somehow, but I appreciated his determination and he proceeded to load his menacing weapon.

As expected, this caused some uneasiness among the others, but when and if the going got tough, it would be me and 2 who would have to deal with it.

*   *   *

One hour later

We left the flat without saying a word. I hoped that everything necessary had been said already. 2 helped 4 to load the two heavy suitcases into the back of the Passat, while I made sure once again that the car was 'clean'. As soon as they got into the car, I positioned the triangle on my Rolex rotating bezel next to the gold dot indicating 2.00; I moved from the kerb and countdown had begun. Peter and 3 followed closely and I drove exactly as I had the day before; I was even wearing my seat belt!

First stop, Pont Street — and first problem!

I had to call Parvez's private line three times before I managed to get an answer and, when this did eventually happen, I immediately recognised Fitzpatrick's voice. At

valerio viccei

first I froze. I did not identify myself and tried hard not to speak with an accent. He told me that Mr Latif was due back any time and that, if I wished to speak to him, I should call back in a few minutes.

I did not panic. I just set my brain to scanning the implications of this unexpected setback. I decided to carry on as scheduled.

Five minutes later I instructed 3 to make his call and query the availability of boxes, plus the possibility of renting one that same afternoon. Fitzpatrick answered the phone and he promptly gave my teammate the information we knew he would offer. 3 made it clear to him that he would be at the Centre, accompanied by his business partner in about twenty minutes. By now the phone box was like a micro-sauna and sweat drenched my immaculate clothes. I tried hard not to lose my calm, but I couldn't ignore the fact that if Parvez did not turn up at the Centre very shortly, it would be pointless for me to carry on with the plan. Five more minutes and the operation would have to be aborted.

For some reason time now seemed to be passing at a much slower pace. When I lifted the phone to dial Parvez's private line again and for the last time, I had to look at my watch twice. It was only five minutes since the last call, but it felt like hours to me.

'Knightsbridge Safety Deposit Centre, can I help you?'

'Parvez, what the hell is going on! Where the fuck were you?'

'Calm down please, everything is fine, my friend. I

had forgotten that the park was going to be closed for a while, so I had to come back by a much longer and busier route. No problem.'

'Hmmmm, I will be there in fifteen minutes . . .'

'I know. I have just been told to expect two potential customers at about that time. I must then assume that everything is fine with you?'

'Well . . . it is now that I have got hold of you, Parvez. You honestly made me sweat, man, but apart from this minor inconvenience everything is under control.' I paused. 'Is it a go then?'

'You are the leader and the decision is yours. Just remember that there is no need to hurt anybody.'

'My word on that, buddy, you must keep calm. We will make it.'

Things were once again moving very fast. When I finally came out of the phone box, the broad smile on my face spoke to the others on my behalf. I did not want to waste words, or any further time at this point; all they got from me was a thumbs-up sign.

We headed for Trevor Square in the knowledge that there was no way back now; only the imponderable could stop this operation from being carried out.

3 was the first to head for his 'spot'. He was in full security guard uniform and had the walkie-talkie professionally clipped to his belt. His instructions were clear. His radio set would be on all the time and he would have to pay particular attention to the volume while he walked up and down the pavement fronting the main entrance of the Centre. He must avoid looking

valerio viccei

through the front door in case he attracted Fitzpatrick's attention. All he had to do was wait for my signal to come in. Once I had secured the entire place I would contact him by radio, and only then should he remove a display on a wooden tripod with the Centre's promotional brochure on it. This was placed right outside the main entrance and was a great nuisance to pedestrians; it also attracted too much attention to a place that, in a few minutes' time, would be taken over by a team of robbers. I wanted the place to look invisible, so the board had to go.

3's next move was to place the display inside the Centre and stick the 'NOTICE TO CUSTOMERS' on the front door's wooden shutters. Once he had accomplished this he would close the shutters from inside, cross the entire length of the ground floor and stick a second label on the outside of the back door.

WE APOLOGISE TO ALL OUR CUSTOMERS FOR ANY INCONVENIENCE CAUSED TO THEM DURING THE IMPROVEMENTS TO OUR SECURITY SYSTEM. BUSINESS AS USUAL FROM TOMORROW THANK YOU

Well, that was what he was supposed to do!

Peter and 4 left next. They carried the two suitcases containing the tools and headed for a pub situated at the intersection between Rutland Street and Fairholt Street. It had a couple of tables outside and at this time of the day it was always deserted.

too fast to live

I entrusted 4 with the walkie-talkie and he, too, would have to wait for my coded message. Once he received the green light, he and Peter would leave their 'spot' and go to the Centre's back entrance, no more than one hundred and fifty metres away. By then I would already be in the control room and, thanks to the Centre's own surveillance system, I would be in a position to let them in as soon as they appeared in front of the video camera hidden inside the intercom. 3 would be at the back door, ready to greet them!

The others had all gone and 2 and I were standing by the Passat looking at each other as if to detect some uneasiness that we could not afford to show in front of them, but there was none and we both pulled faces like only two real friends could in such circumstances. We gripped each other's forearm for a few seconds and then began our short journey, strolling like it was the most natural thing in the world.

The whole area seemed quiet and the day was warm and sunny; I felt just great and, as usual, I was enjoying every single moment. The action was about to begin and that always gave me a real buzz! I felt no fear or remorse, no indecision. My brain was sharp and working fine, my balls were where they were supposed to be and the reassuring weight of the gun in the small of my back and the radio set on my left confirmed to me that this was not a practice any more. This was for real!

We were both dressed extremely smartly in Armani and Kenzo suits, Hermes ties and Ferragamo loafers. We wore gold Rolex wrist watches and designer sunglasses;

221

only the two pilot-cases were ordinary looking, almost anonymous. These are, in fact, the sort of items on which all witnesses, the world over, focus their attention, because that's where money and guns are usually placed just before the robbers leave.

We were standing outside the back door of the Centre. As I was not wearing gloves, I rang the bell using only my fingernail. In a matter of seconds, a metallic click from the electric lock told me that it had been disengaged. This was, in fact, the final step of a long-established security procedure. As soon as the guard in the control room had spotted us through the hidden camera, even before I rang the bell, he had contacted Fitzpatrick by intercom, telling him that two gents were coming in via the back entrance. Having received the all clear from his partner, he would then disengage the lock by pressing one of the many buttons placed next to the monitors.

Having received our call in advance, Fitzpatrick thought we were potential customers, therefore he would immediately have notified Parvez of our arrival. He should appear any time now! Efficiency is always a good sell. The time was 15.10.

If Parvez had decided to set me up, this was the ideal time for the police to close in. If this really was the case, then behind that door there would be at least twenty men from the P17 Unit. I didn't really consider this possibility much at all: my only worry was that Parvez might have lost his bottle already and would come up with a silly excuse.

too fast to live

I slowly pushed the door with my fist and immediately realised that someone was trying to pull it open from inside. It had to be him!

'Good afternoon. I trust you are the gentlemen who made enquiries by phone just a few minutes ago. I am the manager of the Centre.'

I knew that the guard was watching every move we made, as another video camera was just four yards away from where we stood; we were actually facing it. The fact that Parvez was acting his part so well from the beginning made me feel even more confident.

'Yes, we are indeed,' I replied and at the same time I looked straight into his eyes as if to read the mind of this unsettling man. He didn't even blink!

I detected something odd in his smile but assumed it was just tension.

His next few words would establish what was going to happen from now onwards: if he invited us to visit the vaults first, it was a go. Should he take any other initiative, I had to abort the operation.

Come on, say it!

'Please, gentlemen, follow me. I will show you the vaults first and then the whole security set-up. If you are satisfied, we will then discuss the financial aspect of the contract. This way . . .'

Were it not for the video cameras, I would have jumped up and down like a kid: it was working!

We were now covering the few yards separating us from the staircase leading to the basement — a short but extremely dangerous trip. I realised that Fitzpatrick was in

valerio viccei

a position to take a look at us for a brief second and I couldn't let that happen. He knew me very well and one glimpse would be more than enough to fuck everything up. I also knew that his desk fronted the main door; to look in our direction he had to rotate his head at least 140 degrees. As already agreed with both of them, I let Parvez and my partner walk in front of me. They would not turn towards the staircase at the pace they normally used, but much slower and a little further along. In this way I would be shielded from view for the length of time it would take me to reach the first few steps, where I would be safe. As a further precaution, I was already blowing my nose with a handkerchief that entirely covered my face.

We quickly reached the bottom of the staircase where the control room was. In front of us there was an armoured door, on our left a computer with a VDU and, next to it, a large bulletproof glass panel. Behind that I could clearly see the security guard: the real obstacle!

He was new all right and I had never seen him before. Everything was working like a Swiss watch.

Under ordinary circumstances as a client, it was at this point that I would have to insert my code-card in the computer slot, dial my PIN on the keyboard and, if the machine was satisfied, its screen would tell the guard my box number and that all was clear. Only then would the guard release the door's electrical lock. Going through this door I would find myself standing in front of a locked gate protecting the entrance to the vaults themselves: its lock, too, had to be released by the guard in the control

too fast to live

room. During daytime, the function of the gate was to 'substitute' for a massive vault door of a kind that most people would associate with Fort Knox. This now stood wide open next to the gate.

Being with Parvez and acting as potential customers, this procedure did not apply to us, of course, and the guard simply let us through the door first and then, without any delay at all, through the gate. This particular area was controlled by five different video cameras: one was opposite the gate, just outside the vaults, the other four were all inside. I was well aware that if he wished to, the guard could even read my lips. I couldn't afford a single slip or it would all be over before we had a chance to produce our weapons.

We started looking at the boxes, commenting on their size, price and availability. Since he appeared at the back door, I had treated Parvez as a total stranger and I would continue to do so until the end, even when my partners were the only ones around. We walked around very slowly, showing the curiosity that is typical of people who are viewing such a place for the first time. When I thought this play acting had lasted long enough to convince the guard, I walked towards one of the various viewing-closets placed along the cabinets and asked 2 to have a look himself; we exchanged a few comments and only then did I ask Parvez if this was the only kind of viewing room available to the customers. Needless to say, this was not an aimless question, on the contrary it was the key to the whole plan.

There was, in fact, a 'private viewing room' which

was usually used by gold and diamond dealers, or by people who wanted to examine the contents of their boxes in total privacy and needed more space. This room led to a further section of the basement, the 'storage room', where the largest items were kept, outside the boxes, but in a secure area covered by increased alarm protection. A fly couldn't get in there!

The peculiarity of the private viewing room was that it was the only part of the whole basement not covered by video cameras. Once we were in there, the guard could only guess what was going on and Parvez would be under my complete control. Nobody would ever be in a position to challenge his reconstruction of events and of what had taken place inside it. Besides, he would relate exactly what had happened and that was one of the reasons why I would treat him as a true victim all along. That way we wouldn't fuck up.

'No, actually we have a further facility for the customers who want to examine the contents of their boxes in complete privacy and for as long as they wish.'

'Could we have a look at it, please?'

'Sure. Please follow me.'

He opened the door to the room and held it so that my partner and I could walk in first, disappearing from the monitors.

As soon as he, too, walked in, I shut the door. I laid my pilot-case on top of one of the two tables, as did my partner; nobody said a word. I swiftly slipped behind Parvez, took my gun out and grabbed him by the neck! I gently pushed him towards the nearest chair and told him

too fast to live

to sit down. He looked shocked. This was for real, no rehearsal could have prepared him for what was happening.

'Don't say a word. Just relax and listen to me very carefully. We will now walk back towards the control room and, once we are out of the vaults, you will reach for the phone on the table opposite the gate. Geddit? Now, you will call the guard in the control room and this is what you will tell him. Pay full attention and memorise this correctly for your own sake.'

'I will do anything you say, you don't need to hurt me.'

'I know that what you ask him to do has been done in the past, so make sure that your guard will comply with your request or you are going to regret it. Is that understood, Mr Latif?'

'Yes, yes . . . Mr Digney will comply with my request immediately as long as you don't act in a suspicious way. He has no reason to suspect that something is wrong, but we'd better leave this room as soon as possible.'

Out of my pilot-case I took a long section of stainless steel chain and then a padlock with which I secured the chain around a concrete pillar. I also took out two sets of handcuffs and a pair of gloves which disappeared into my jacket pockets. We were now ready to go and this little break had given Parvez the chance to regain his composure. He looked calm.

Before we left the room I spoke to him again, as too much self-confidence could lead to serious mistakes on his part.

valerio viccei

'You will say only what I have told you to say. If he becomes suspicious and doesn't comply with your request, you are going to be very sorry, pal. Let's go now.'

I replaced the gun in the back of my waistband and told my partner to open the door. He hadn't said a single word, but his facial expression would have frightened a corpse! We left.

Until now everything had been perfect, timing and all, but I knew that the real business had yet to begin. Only when Mr Digney was within my reach would I finally be able to relax. At the moment we were still divided by armoured doors, bulletproof glass and a gate; a mere twenty yards can still represent a long, long way. As soon as we were through the gate, Parvez reached for the phone and dialled.

'Mr Digney, these gentlemen would like to be shown what happens if someone should turn up and try to gain access to a box simply by using the key and the card which the owner may have lost. Do you mind showing them why such an attempt would be pointless and doomed to failure?'

'No problem, Sir.'

When I heard the first of the two doors unlock, my heartbeat increased slightly. I discreetly checked the time: 15.15. Perfect timing once again! One more door, one more 'click' and the next obstacle would be within arm's length: the Centre would soon be mine for two long hours.

At the moment we were still sandwiched between two armoured doors but unless a client came in now there was no reason why our friend Digney should not open the last door.

Had it come from a 200-watt Bose speaker, the last 'click' could have not sounded louder to me. Parvez opened the door and I was finally walking into the guard's lair, my senses more alert than they had ever been.

The room was extremely cramped and there were so many monitors, electrical panels, buttons, switches, phones and other hi-tech paraphernalia that I was quite impressed. I knew exactly where the panic button was, but I wasn't prepared for such a tiny room: it was so small that 2 had to wait on the threshold and Parvez was dangerously close to some control panels that were supplementary to the main one. If there was a struggle something could go off by mistake. Flexibility had played a big role in my plan, thank God, but I was now facing a situation I hadn't reckoned on. I couldn't take chances.

Unseen by the guard I gestured to my partner to keep outside the door and for Latif to move away from where he was. At the same time I moved closer to the guard who was by now mumbling something about codes and numbers, computers and locks. I was right behind his chair, trying to give him the impression that I was concentrating hard on what he was saying. I was so close that I could smell his sweat, but the control panel was easily within his reach and only a powerful blow delivered with the butt of my gun would put him in a condition in which he could not react. I didn't want to hurt him, I didn't want to resort to violence at all, let alone spill any blood if it could be avoided. The man had done nothing

valerio viccei

to me and this was his job, but I also had a strict schedule to observe and if I didn't come up with a better idea within seconds, I would have to knock him unconscious.

He was still seated. I was standing so close to him that I realised that I could easily press my cock against his right upper arm. As I had hoped, the man was not gay and he found what I was doing extremely embarrassing. He quickly withdrew his arm, but I did not give up and prayed that he would do exactly what I would do in the same circumstances. He did!

Digney looked at me with an embarrassed expression and pushed his chair back a few inches. Then he slowly got up, still mumbling about security and pointing one finger towards the computer screen.

My left hand was as quick as a cat's paw reaching for a mouse. Before he realised what was happening, I pulled him out of the room. At the same time the gun appeared in my right hand, level with his neck, its barrel pressing the flesh. It was all over; leg 4 was completed.

Digney was a man of average build and, at that moment, a very frightened one as well; this made things a lot easier for everybody. Not that it would have made a lot of difference, but the fact that I could easily manhandle him was a psychological barrier that prevented him even from thinking about reacting. He kept staring at Parvez as if he could tell him what the hell was going on. Had he had any doubts, my partner's sawn-off shotgun, by now aimed at his boss's head, must have convinced him that the two of them were in deep trouble.

The whole thing had been extremely quick and we

too fast to live

had spent no more than a couple of minutes in the control room.

'Don't move. Don't even breathe, or you will regret it, pal! Now get down on the floor very slowly and keep your hands above your head. Good, that's a good man. Put them behind your back. That's fine.'

Then, addressing my partner, I added: 'Jack, if the punk makes a move, just blow his legs off right away and he won't bother us any more!'

Obviously I didn't mean it in the slightest, but I now had to handcuff the poor bastard and that implied putting my gun away. I didn't want Digney to do anything silly as then I would have to beat him senseless. If a little threat could help to prevent trouble, all the better.

Number 2 worked like a machine, silent and efficient. Even as I noted this, I couldn't help thinking about the others, which simply gave me goose bumps!

'OK, buddy, you are in the bag now and my advice to you is that you'd better be a good boy for a while, or you and Mr Latif here are going to suffer. What do you say?'

'I am new here; I don't know nothing. Please don't hurt me.'

'Calm down, buddy. Nobody is going to harm you as long as you do as you are told. Is that a deal or what?'

'Sure . . . whatever you say.'

'All right, then, get up. You are going to be chained to the pillar inside the viewing room, but you won't be on your own too long. Soon your colleague and this gentleman here will be keeping you company, Let's go — now!'

valerio viccei

All three of the doors and the gate were self-locking and I was extremely concerned that one of them would get shut by accident; this would cause unmentionable problems, so before we left the control room I wanted to make sure that its door, and all the others, would be kept open by means of plastic doorstops we had brought with us. They were tricky little things and kept sliding about all the time, especially on the carpet. In the end we decided to forget about the doorstops and use some folded newspapers and a chair instead. You can't beat a good old chair when it comes to keeping a heavy door open!

I left for the viewing room, dragging Digney along, while Parvez was guarded by 2. When I reached the room I secured Digney to the chain with the handcuffs. Next I got rid of the two internal telephones even though I knew he would never be in a position to reach them.

'Are they too tight, buddy?'

'No they are fine. Thanks.'

'You need anything?'

'Could I kick my shoes off?'

'Sure you can, as long as the other two don't complain. And what about loosening your tie?'

'Yes, please.'

I left Digney and ran back to where the other two were waiting for me. They were just outside the control room. It was time to get Fitzpatrick and I wanted to do it as soon as possible.

15.20 — things looked good!

too fast to live

The basement was secured, the various doors and the gate were wide open. One more obstacle and the whole Centre would belong to us. I gave the thumbs-up sign to my partner and told him to replace the sawn-off shotgun in his pilot-case. I also pushed Parvez towards the staircase and told him that we were going to his office. As I didn't want to be seen by the other guard, he and my man would have to walk in front of me, acting as a screen.

My handkerchief was once again covering part of my face. As soon as he heard our footsteps, Fitzpatrick turned round very slowly and without paying too much attention. The sight of Parvez must have satisfied the natural suspicion that goes with his job because he quickly returned to his paperback.

I slipped inside Parvez's office unseen by the guard and was soon followed by the other two. I shut the door carefully; the worst part was over. I told Parvez to call Fitzpatrick on his internal telephone and ask him to get some brochures for us. He picked up the phone immediately and dialled a short number. My partner got out the sawn-off shotgun again and hid it under his jacket, his back to the door behind which I was now standing, gun in hand and wearing a balaclava.

A knock on the door. 'Mr Latif . . .?'

I nodded, and Parvez replied: 'Yes, John, come in.

The guard had not come two steps into the room before I grabbed him by the neck with my left hand. At the same time I positioned myself between him and the door in order to cut off any possible retreat. All he could see was a red balaclava, but my gun and the sawn-off shotgun, now aimed at his boss's chest, must have convinced him that he had better be careful, very careful indeed.

'Get down! Get down, you son of a bitch!'

'Yes, but don't shoot . . .'

He lay on the floor, belly-down, and I sat on his bum. Before I handcuffed him, I levelled my Beretta against his face and, very dramatically, pulled its slide half-way back to expose the shining brass shell in the chamber. I wanted him to be certain that, if things turned nasty, people could get seriously hurt.

'Right, John, the game is up as far as you are concerned. I am in charge of this place now. Do exactly as you are told and everything will be fine. Is that understood?'

'Understood. I won't do anything unless you ask me to.'

'Leader to number 3 . . . Leader to number 3 . . . Take-over completed, come in now. I repeat, come in now.'

2 and I had performed our tasks swiftly and efficiently; the sooner 3 shut the whole place down, the sooner I could contact Peter and 4 who, by now, must have heard that leg 5 had been successfully completed. I waited but there was no confirmation from 3.

'Leader to 3 . . . Leader to 3 . . .' I repeated. 'It is all clear for you to come in. Have you copied? Confirm it.' I said again into my radio mike, hardly suppressing my increasing apprehension.

Still nothing.

too fast to live

'Number 3, you asshole! Give me an answer and come in immediately!!!'

By now I was shouting my head off and I bet he could have heard me even without the aid of the radio speaker. I was becoming furious, with the result that the atmosphere was highly volatile. My worst fears were coming true; those wankers outside were screwing everything up.

I swore to myself that if such a thing happened and I walked out in one piece, I would shoot them all. I honestly would!

I couldn't believe it! Clients could walk in at any time. They would notice immediately that the Centre was unmanned. They would probably run off and tell the first policeman they came across. Shit!

Fitzpatrick was shaking like a washing machine, perhaps thinking that I was going to work out my murderous rage on him. He had nothing to fear, of course, I wouldn't dream of doing such a thing, but I couldn't blame the man for getting scared as I was getting really mad.

For the first time since we set foot inside the Centre 2 spoke, which startled me.

'Calm down, just calm down for a second. I'm gonna fetch that son of a bitch, but don't you blow your top. We can still make it.'

I was a bit sceptical about this, but I also knew that we were running out of time and that the doors had to be shut immediately. 2 could do it himself.

I looked at Parvez who by now seemed to be as

valerio viccei

frightened as the guard. When he was sure that Fitzpatrick was not in a position to see him, he pointed a finger at my partner and nodded very slowly. 2 smiled, placed the shotgun on top of the table, and headed for the front door. He now knew who my inside man was.

Still no answer from 3. The time was 15.37.

Suddenly a startling loud buzzer went off, nearly giving us all heart failure.

'What the fuck was that?' I shouted at the top of my voice, making the guard jump like a startled rabbit.

'The alarm . . .'

'What?'

'. . . the alarm has gone off but . . .'

Only then did I notice that Parvez was trying to attract my attention, but the dreadful noise, amplified by the unnatural silence surrounding the place, was driving me insane and making me think the worst. I felt I was losing control and I was on my own, totally cut off from the rest of the team. Where was 2? What sort of alarm was this and who had set it off?

'It is nothing, believe me, Sir . . .' Parvez mumbled totally stricken with fear. 'It is simply a very loud buzzer activated by someone standing on the doormat, the one in between the wooden shutters and the glass front door. It could be a client, but it might also be your friend. Please don't shoot us.'

'You go and have a look! If it is my friend let him in. The same applies if it is a client, but if you make a wrong move I will shoot your guard here. Is that clear, Latif?'

Fitzpatrick was handcuffed behind his back and still

too fast to live

lay on his belly so I could afford to move away from him and watch Parvez. I immediately recognised 2 and 3, both standing on the bloody doormat. The noise stopped as soon as they came in.

The wooden shutters appeared to be closed and the promotional display rested next to them. I could breathe again, but I could hardly control the temptation to beat the living daylights out of 3. I called him the worst names I could think of, but all he did was point at the radio set as if it was to blame. I took a closer look; the volume indicator showed that the idiot had been walking along the Old Brompton Road with an almost silent speaker. How could he ever have hoped to hear me, the fool.

I told him as much, but the punk was clearly wetting his trousers and unable to speak. There was still a lot to do and we were behind schedule; I still had to deal with the handcuffed guard in Parvez's office and tell Peter and 4 to come in. I couldn't waste any more time on 3, so I told him to get to the back door and finish his job without screwing things up any further. I then lifted the terrorised Fitzpatrick off the floor and dragged him towards the staircase leading to the vaults. I told him to move his ass because I was going to handcuff him to his pal Digney and leave them alone for a while. He was glad to hear it.

* * *

Both the front and the back doors were now shut, and notices had been placed on the outsides as planned. This,

valerio viccei

added to the fact that Digney and Fitzpatrick were locked away in the viewing room and handcuffed to the concrete pillar, gave me total control of the entire Centre. Unless I wanted them to, nobody could get in and nobody could get out!

By now, Parvez knew that he had given himself away to my colleague and that our pretence was completely pointless. This notwithstanding, I didn't want him to relax too much as the guards might well detect something odd in the way he was reacting to his ordeal. I told him to stay in his office and go about his business without interfering with ours. Besides, he would have to answer any incoming phone calls from clients who might have become a little worried at this sudden need for security improvements. I would continue to boss him around whenever my teammates were near us, of course, but we both understood the futility of such behaviour.

'Leader to 4, you have permission to move in. Over.'

The following seconds seemed like eternity to me again, but my radio speaker was as dead as ever. Even the usual static background was totally quiet. Murderous rage was engulfing my being as I calculated all the possible implications of this further setback. There was only one option.

'Leader to 4 . . . Leader to 4 . . .' I tried over and over again, cursing him and his mother, his father and his forebearer with such forcefulness that 3 got quickly out of the way and out of my reach.

I suddenly took my balaclava off and wiped the sweat off my face. Things had been so hectic that I had

too fast to live

forgotten to get rid of the damn thing after locking Fitzpatrick in the viewing room.

I needed to sit and think.

I swore like there was no tomorrow to get the anger off my chest, but this had a bad effect on the others; even 2 seemed a little uneasy.

I got up from the chair, grabbed 3's radio, double checked that the frequency and volume were set correctly, then I passed it to 2.

'I can only hope that those two idiots on the outside haven't left for good and that the problem is only communications again. Anyway, I am going out to look for them; is that OK with you, buddy?'

'Sure it is!'

'I will let you know what is going on out there, but I won't say a word on the radio. I will just squeeze the call--button pad five times if they are still there, twice if they are not. I'll be back no matter what, but if I should shout "Run" into the mike, you'll know that it's all over. You must confirm at once, and in the same way, that you have copied my message. Geddit?'

'Sure, man. No sweat!'

'Can you handle this lot?'

'Sure. No problem! Just get on with it and good luck, brother.'

Before I left I checked my gun for the umpteenth time in ten minutes. I clipped my walkie-talkie to my trouser belt, and took a long breath. I would not admit to failure as yet, but I knew that things looked very bad indeed. If those two assholes were not where they were

valerio viccei

supposed to be, it would all be over in a matter of minutes.

I opened the back door. As soon as I stepped outside, I literally bumped into a fully uniformed policeman!

'Good afternoon,' is all I could think of saying, while my right hand automatically felt for the butt of my Beretta and I prepared myself for a shoot out.

'Good afternoon to you, too,' was his reply. He didn't pay any more attention to me than a busy dustman would!

Mechanically I crossed Cheval Place, looking left first. All was clear from that direction but as soon as I started checking the other side I almost broke into a run. At the intersection with Montpelier Street I could clearly make out at least three police vehicles surrounded by uniformed cops.

I checked once more what the copper was up to, but the bugger was simply walking down the street on his own. To my experienced eye, he appeared too relaxed to have anything to do with my business at the Centre. What should I do now? My instinct told me that this huge police presence was due to some other business, but who could tell! Should I shout 'run' into the mike and give my two partners a chance to escape now, or follow my intuition instead? It was a tough decision and one which, one way or the other, I might regret for ever. I closed my eyes for a fraction of a second and prayed that I was doing the right thing. I walked on!

* * *

too fast to live

There the two bums were. Chatting and laughing like two old ladies at a friend's birthday party.

'Hi, Gi! Anything wrong?' Peter said in his broad Cockney accent.

I didn't say a word and my expression must have told them that everything was wrong! They looked at each other and then in the direction of the walkie-talkie hidden under 4's jacket. There was no one around, thank God, and not a trace of the swarming cops. I told 4 not to touch his radio, then I calmly squeezed the squelch-pad of my own set five times. Those at the Centre could now relax a little and, in fact, I immediately got 2's acknowledgement: bip . . . bip . . . bip . . . bip . . . bip . . . Good man!

As if to confirm my suspicions, 4's radio had remained silent all along with no trace of these last two communications from its speaker! Peter and 4 knew very well that they had fucked up; they didn't say a word and just held their breath. I tucked my hand under 4's jacket and reached for his radio set; I unclipped it from the belt and took a good look at it. Somehow, the idiot had managed to change the pre-set frequency and this was why even my call-signal sent from two yards away could not be received. I had to resist the temptation to punch him in the mouth, but my bitterness was more than evident.

'Sorry, Gigi . . . I don't know how it happened,' he said.

'Forget it!'

'But why are you still outside, is something wrong?'

'What am I doing outside, uh? You miserable cunt, I

valerio viccei

have just left the other two lads inside and come out to look for you two and you ask me why I am outside?'

'I don't understand honestly. What do you mean by that?'

'I mean, you son of a bitch, that everything has been done. We are all safely in and now I have had to come out here looking for you two. Now move your ass and let's get out of here.'

'You can't be serious! What do you mean "everything has been done"?' Peter asked.

'I am saying that I have got the two guards already chained up and that the whole Centre was secured fifteen minutes ago, you asshole, but unless you bring those two suitcases inside, we can't start. Now move!!'

They both got up at once looking flabbergasted. Very likely the wankers had hoped I wouldn't make it. Now they realised that the 'dance' was about to begin for them too. They looked a bit pale.

I did not mention the bit about the police in case they ran like scared rabbits. I only hoped that the coast was clear. Once we had turned the corner and reached Cheval Place, we would be only fifteen yards from the back door of the Centre — too late for them to back off. Besides, I would never have let them go. Only over my dead body!

As if miracles were possible, the police vehicles had moved away and where, just a few minutes earlier, there had been dozens, I couldn't see a single uniform. I was so goddamned glad that I grinned like a happy little kid. I even got so cocky that I pressed the mike-pad and said softly, 'Open up, buddy, we're coming in.'

The door opened very slowly and when we walked in the street was totally deserted — finally I had with me all the equipment I needed. Now everything was fine and the nightmare was over. It would be downhill all the way, I had no doubt about that. The time was 15.45.

Parvez was still in his office and I told him that we were finally in a position to start. I felt like apologising for the various cock-ups and the disgraceful performance of my team, but it would be pointless and totally unfair to 2 who, once again, had not disappointed me.

In a few minutes I was going to chain Parvez to the pillar, as already agreed, so I wanted to make sure that I knew all I needed to know and that things like the doormat business wouldn't happen again. By now, the guards might well be wondering why he was not being treated in the same way as them, so it was essential that the three of them should share the same conditions of captivity for some time. It wouldn't be for too long, as I had already planned to get him out of the viewing room again in about ten minutes, but it had to be done none the less. By then he would be able to tell me what the guards thought of the whole business and if, by any chance, Fitzpatrick had recognised me. You never know with security guards!

I needed Parvez back as soon as possible for two reasons: he would have to answer all incoming phone calls and, at the same time, keep an eye on the monitors connected to the outside video cameras. This would give me an extra man and at this stage of the plan I needed all the co-operation I could get from my partners. The work was now only manual, so the risk of someone screwing things up again was very limited indeed.

I put my balaclava back on and opened the viewing room door very slowly. The two guards were sitting with their backs against the pillar and seemed relaxed, at least they did not show any apparent sign of anxiety or hyperventilation. Fitzpatrick was the one who managed to handle the situation with most dignity, but he never dared to look in my direction.

'How you doing, buddies?'

'All right,' they both replied.

'Need anything?'

They shook their heads, but I checked the handcuffs all the same, only to find out that they were already pretty loose. I then walked outside and, after a few seconds, came back with Parvez with my gun aimed at his head and my manners very rude. I handcuffed him to the chain and left the room without saying a word.

CHAPTER 10

Aladdin's Cave

The suitcases had been relieved of their heavy contents and all the equipment was neatly displayed on the vault floor, just opposite the gate. The various electrical tools, grinding machines and powerful drills had already been connected to the power points, their extension leads crisscrossing the room. Seeing the huge screwdrivers, the crow bars and the rest of the material so tidily arranged made me feel better than I had felt since we left 3's flat. A demonstration of efficiency at long last, and about time too!

We were all wearing gloves, of course, while my balaclava was off once again. This was an unplanned pause which seemed to be welcome to all of us, but I couldn't afford to waste a single minute and now I had to make up my mind how I would start. We had several

valerio viccei

options in theory, but the time factor had now become paramount and some of them would have to be put aside. My hesitation lasted just a few seconds then I suddenly bent down and reached for the custom-made sledgehammer. I balanced its reassuring weight carefully and took a deep breath, then I turned to face the rows of boxes on my left.

The first blow was devastating and the noise of steel against steel was as deafening as thunder! I missed the lock by less than half an inch, but the impact was so powerful that I bent the reddish-coated door as if it were a can of Coke. The second layer of steel, painted blue, was now clearly visible and was the only obstacle between me and the plastic box housed behind it. The lads came forward brandishing all sort of tools and it was evident to everybody that they would have had an easy task finishing the job but I wanted to do it myself.

I raised my left hand and gestured to them to hold their horses. Two more powerful blows, this time hitting the lock with deadly precision, crushed the lot to an unrecognisable piece of junk. Cheers filled the room. By now, my excitement was growing: adrenalin was pumping hard. I dropped the sledgehammer on the floor and, with studied care, I removed the metallic debris, grabbed the huge plastic container with both hands and pulled it from the recess. The box, being some 15 x 15 x 25 inches, was the biggest size available to the clients: its weight was staggering! I laid it on the floor and slowly lifted its flap.

Everybody moved nearer in anticipation. I dug my

too fast to live

hands in and grabbed thick bundles of neatly stacked bank notes, all of them brand-new fifties and twenties. Next came gold watches, designer necklaces, rings with precious stones and many, many leather pouches whose contents would remain a mystery for a few more hours. A quick, mental calculation of what I was looking at told me that my big hammer had already made me a millionaire.

I closed my eyes for a second and shook my head as if in disbelief: it had worked! I told 2 to fetch one of the large plastic bags still lying on the floor and to make sure that all the cash ended up in it. His duty would consist of looking after this particular bag until we left. Should things go wrong, we would at least try to carry the bag with us. The rest would be much too heavy to handle under similar circumstances. He winked and made no comment, but I could tell he was happy with my decision.

I also instructed Peter and 3 to fill the other bags with everything other than silverware, documents and 'awkward' stuff. I would quickly go through what they discarded when we were finished, just in case, but I already knew that we wouldn't need any of it. We were going only for the cream!

I told 4 to stuff three different tools in his waistband and follow me. The technique I had opted for was a very simple one. I would smash locks and doors; 4 would complete the job and get the debris out of the way, Peter and 3 would sort the stuff and fill the green bags. We couldn't go wrong!

The pace was very fast and tiring but we managed to

carry on non-stop for almost half an hour. Two of the bags were already full.

Then, 'Bingo! . . . Look at this, guys!' shouted 3.

It was breathtaking! One of the boxes we had just smashed open lay at his feet, its flap lifted. The container was filled to the brim with US bank notes: all new $100 bills in wads of 500. I am not that good with numbers, but I calculated that this little lot must be worth well over half a million!

Next it was Peter's turn to shout with joy. He was holding in his hand what looked like a huge rock of pink cocaine, its probable weight not less than a kilo. In another box next to him there was more of it and also about £200,000, all in new fifty-pound notes. Things were looking very good indeed.

I told the lads to take a rest and to get away from the viewing room door because I was going to let Parvez out and I didn't want the guards to see any of them. 4 objected saying that he had never been seen by Parvez either and he would like things to stay that way. It was a good point and I agreed with him that he should hide somewhere for the short while I needed to bring Parvez into the control room.

By now, of course, everybody knew who my inside man was, but things could still go wrong and we didn't know how Parvez would react. I did not want to risk him seeing 4.

I put my balaclava on again and opened the door. The captives were all very quiet and showed no sign of stress so far.

too fast to live

'Hey you! What time do you think the supervisor is coming today?'

'Difficult to say, Sundays are very peculiar days for him, but usually it is between 5.15 and 5.45,' Parvez said very slowly.

'Don't you fuck with me, Paki, or you gonna regret it!'

'Honestly, I am telling the truth. Why should I lie to you? You can ask the guards here. They will tell you.'

I looked in Fitzpatrick's direction and asked him the same question.

'Mr Latif's right, Sir. He'll arrive between 5.15 and a quarter to six.'

'Will he be on his own?'

'Well, he usually is and . . .'

'Cut the crap, buddy, I wanna hear clear answers. No bullshit!'

This time it was Parvez who volunteered the information, but my question was intended to show that my knowledge of the security arrangements was pretty poor so that, consequently, this would be reported to the police. 'Yes, the supervisor will be on his own unless something very serious has happened during his afternoon rounds. And that doesn't happen very often.'

'Good man. Now I am going to take you to the control room, boss, and you will give me some more information or I'll blow your head off there and then. Come on, turn round.'

I freed him from the handcuffs and led him out of the room at gunpoint. I shut the door behind us and then gave him my best smile. I placed my right finger against my lips to intimate to him to keep quiet and, at the same time, I pushed him towards the control room, calling him names very loudly.

Once we were in the room I noticed that Parvez looked a little shaky and pale. He asked me if he could use the loo. He came back quickly and started asking me all sorts of questions. I reassured him, saying that everything was fine and that we already had a few million in our pockets. He smiled.

I wanted to know if the guards had made any comment or given him the impression that they suspected anybody in particular. He said that neither of them had spoken a single word. They had only exchanged glances and gestures, but from what he had understood the poor bastards hadn't even got a clue how many of us there were.

I told him that as we were short of time I couldn't afford to have one of my men sitting in front of the monitors all the time; it would be handy if he could do that for me. Besides, he would also be in a position to answer the phone immediately. Things looked good at the moment, but you never knew and the longer we stayed, the more the risk that a suspicious client might turn up and decide to call the Centre to check would increase. He said that it was fine with him.

We could start again. It was 16.20.

* * *

too fast to live

We had been working non-stop for about twenty minutes and I had to admit that everybody was being efficient, even 3 and Peter had managed to sort the stuff with a degree of accuracy that quite surprised me. I kept an eye on my watch and, from time to time, I would pop into the control room and check how Parvez was doing. Everything was fine.

My right arm was now in terrible pain from the strain caused by lifting the heavy sledgehammer hundreds of times and suffering its recoil. Eventually, it started to hamper my physical performance. I was drenched in sweat and I felt I needed a little rest but I was also battling against time and it was hard to call for a break now that things were looking so good.

All of a sudden Parvez came rushing towards the vaults and we all jumped as if hit by a live cable!

'The telephone . . . someone is calling! What shall I do?'

I immediately noticed a change of mood among the rest of the team. Apart from 2, everybody seemed struck dumb by fear. I kept calm.

'Well, go and answer it, you dummy, why do you think I asked you to sit there?'

He rushed back towards the control room and I followed him, still carrying the hammer with me; it had almost become an extension of my body. His hand was on the phone, ready to lift it, but I quickly placed mine on top of it and looked straight into his eyes.

'Slow down and be calm. It could be anybody, even the police, but it doesn't necessarily mean that they know what's happening down here. Do not lose control. Say exactly what you have to say. We have been through this over and over again, my friend. Please don't let me down.'

'Knightsbridge Safe Deposit Centre, can I help you?'

I couldn't hear what was being said at the other end of the line, but Parvez's expression relaxed and that meant things couldn't be that bad.

'Yes, I appreciate that, Sir, and I understand your concern . . . No, in fact it wasn't our initiative at all, but the insurance company wanted to be covered and we had to comply . . . only a further precaution that's all.'

Whoever was on the phone was still talking, but from what I could understand it was simply a suspicious client asking for an explanation as to why the Centre had been shut down at such short notice.

'Yes, from tomorrow everything is back to normal, Sir. I apologise again for the inconvenience, but it was unavoidable . . . Thank you for calling.'

He put the phone down and breathed heavily for a short while, but I had to know what it was all about immediately. In this business there is no room for compassion, I am afraid, and the job was far from completed.

'Phew . . . just a client who wanted to know if everything was fine. You may have guessed that much. I assume he wasn't too suspicious otherwise he would have asked to speak to one of the guards too; what do you think?'

'Good point, Parvez, but do you know him personally?'

too fast to live

'Yes, I think so and if I am right the man is a very ordinary one, nothing unusual about him.'

'What's your personal impression? Do you think he swallowed it?'

'Hook, line and sinker.'

'Hope you are right, buddy, or we are done for. I have to go back there now . . . Oh shit !'

I was staring at my right hand. Parvez stared too. The glove was torn in two different places and blood oozed from what must be quite a large gash. The right sleeve of my white shirt was stained red and I could feel the sticky dampness inside the glove increasing by the minute. It must have happened at some time while I was smashing the locks. The strain of wielding the hammer and the tension of the occasion had blocked out the pain.

I looked more closely at the mess, only to discover that one of my fingertips was no longer protected by the glove. The gash looked a bit ugly, but what terrified me was the tear in the glove; its implications were immense.

I swore aloud and ran towards the vaults where everybody was still waiting to hear about the phone call. Now that I was looking for them, it was not difficult to spot little bloodstains everywhere: on the carpet, boxes, tools, you name it. I quickly put the balaclava on and opened the viewing door — there were stains even on the guards' shirts!

Unless I decided to burn the whole place down there was nothing I could do about this botch and it would be pointless to think otherwise! Things like this do happen and it was tough luck that it had happened to me during the most important operation of my life.

I left the room, taking both gloves off as I went. By now, my fingerprints must be everywhere. I tore my handkerchief up and tied it tightly around the wound. That would do for the time being.

I went to get Parvez out of the control room. I told him that I would have to put him back with the guards, adding that I would speak to him again just before I left. We would have to call it a day very soon. We were running out of time and I wanted to be ready for the supervisor. Parvez said that that was fine with him.

The minutes seemed to fly. While I was still hitting the boxes like a man possessed, I heard Peter say that it was 5.00 pm. Time to stop. I quickly went through the stuff scattered on the floor but was satisfied that the lads had followed my instructions to the letter. The mess was total! 2 was grinning and coughing loudly, his eyes shining with delight. 'Come here, pal, and take a look at this!' he said almost in a whisper. The huge bag, which he was still dragging around as though it was a naughty big dog, was half full; he could hardly lift it. I took it from him and thrust my hands inside, feeling the thick bundles of bank notes in many different currencies. One of the wads was about six inches high and made up of 1,000 Swiss franc notes held together by elastic bands. I slapped 2 heavily on the back and shook my head in disbelief.

'Right, I want all the tools back in the suitcases and all the green bags lined up next to the back door. Also make sure that nothing is hanging out of them and that

too fast to live

there are no holes. Once you are finished, try to make yourselves look presentable. You are going straight to the airport. Here is some pocket money for the first few days,' I said, digging my hands inside the bag of cash, and taking out four bundles of brand-new fifty-pound notes. Each bundle was protected by a sealed plastic bag still bearing the logo of the National Westminster Bank and totalling £2,500. They pocketed the money with grins of satisfaction and quickly returned to their tasks. I went one more time through the green bag and dug out more bundles of new fifties; I had not forgotten about Parvez's briefcase still waiting for me in his office. Once I had put together about £40,000, I ran upstairs and placed the money inside the two large manila envelopes. I sealed them, closed the briefcase and locked the combination!

On my way back to the vaults, I bumped into 2 and 3 who appeared to be struggling with one of the bags filled with loot. From the strain and sweat on their faces, I assumed that the weight must be enormous; I was glad that I had tested the bags repeatedly and that the time spent looking for that particular type of bag had proved a good investment.

From the viewing room there was total silence. Now that all the banging and crashing had suddenly stopped, the atmosphere was pretty unreal and I wondered what the guards must be thinking. They knew their supervisor was about to arrive and that if we managed to overpower him the last obstacle to the successful achievement of our operation would be removed. Were they thinking we might waste them all in order to eliminate witnesses?

valerio viccei

I put the balaclava on for the umpteenth time and I slowly opened the door of the viewing room.

'Everything's done, buddies, but don't worry. Once I have got hold of the supervisor, I shall bring him down here and chain him to the pillar as well. Nobody will get harmed in any way; you with me?'

'Yes, thank you,' said Fitzpatrick, followed by Digney and Parvez. They looked relieved and I was glad that a few words had helped to make them feel better. Who knows what sorts of dreadful thoughts must have crossed their minds in the last two hours?

I walked towards Parvez, grabbed his handcuffs and unlocked them. Without saying a word I dragged him out of the room and, after I had made sure that the door was firmly shut behind us, I started briefing him about the latest developments. I didn't forget to tell him about the present in his briefcase! He asked me if everything was OK and if I felt that overpowering the supervisor might be a tricky business. If a wolf could smile then that's what I must have looked like to him.

Apart from 2, everybody else was upstairs trying to line the bags against the wall so that they wouldn't look too suspicious to the supervisor, at least for the milliseconds preceding my strike! As a further precaution, I asked Parvez to show 2 which button would release the back door and how to keep the monitor tuned on the video camera overlooking that area. While I would be hiding inside the meter room, ready to jump the supervisor, 2 would wait in the control room and let him in. I told Parvez that the man could arrive any time now,

too fast to live

so I'd better put him back with the two guards. He wished me luck and headed once again towards the viewing room; I followed him closely.

'When you hear the bell and see the fucker appear on this monitor, give me five seconds and then press the button, geddit?' I told 2.

'No problem, buddy.'

'Don't fuck it up now, old man, or it's all over. You understand that?'

He didn't reply, he just pulled a face and motioned me to go. The man was solid gold; I left the control room feeling relaxed.

They were the longest five minutes of my life. I was surrounded by nine huge bags containing incalculable treasure and millions of pounds in cash; my white Renault van was parked just opposite the door behind which I was hiding and still I had to wait!

I heard his car the same way a dog can recognise the car belonging to its owner. What followed played in my mind at slow speed: the car door opened and shut, quick footsteps headed for the Centre's back entrance, finally the bell rang — two clear, short rings! I silently counted the seconds, then 'click!', 2 had released the door lock!

The man was inside! I could see him from the dark of the tiny room where I was hiding like a vampire ready to strike. I waited for the door to lock itself, then the poor bastard would be cut off from the rest of the world. 'Click!'

Wearing my red balaclava, I sprang from my lair shouting something unintelligible and grabbed him from behind. He didn't see the gun in my hand, there was not time. He was overwhelmed by shock

'Down! Get down and don't move!'

I prayed for his own sake that he had already realised any reaction on his part would be followed by painful retribution. He had indeed!

I took the handcuffs out of my pocket and put them on him as I had done with the other two guards, securing his arms behind his back. By the time he was chained up next to Parvez and his colleagues, the little viewing room looked pretty cramped but my four captives did not seem to be concerned about it. All they wanted was to see the back of me and my partners as soon as possible.

'You, supervisor, what time will they start looking for you?'

'I usually call headquarters after I have completed setting the alarms and shutting the place down, say anything between thirty and forty minutes after I leave the car.'

'What will happen then, I mean once they realise that you have failed to call within a reasonable time?'

'They'll try to contact me on the car phone and if there is no reply they will call the Centre. Calling the police is the last of all options open to them.'

'What is that thing strapped to your belt?' I asked the man, who appeared to be genuinely puzzled.

'Do you mean the bleeper?'

'I want to know how it works and don't even try to be clever with me as you wouldn't live long enough to congratulate yourself.'

too fast to live

'All right, it's like an ordinary British Telecom pager . . .'

'Fuck British Telecom, buddy, all I want to know is if it works as a transmitter as well; you know what I mean, don't you?'

'Oh, I see! No way, mister, you can have a look yourself. There's no call button . . . nothing at all,' he said.

I took it and looked at it carefully. I was satisfied that the strange object was not a silent distress-call transmitter but I wanted to know more from this guy who was definitely much cooler than the other two guards.

'Are you saying that once this thing goes off, it means that your controller is getting edgy?'

'That's one way to put it, mister, but you would still have ten minutes before all hell breaks loose. I mean before control notifies the police.'

Good. Unless these bums freed themselves too early, which they wouldn't, my escape route would be totally safe for well over half an hour. By then my white Renault van would be unobtrusively parked in front of an anonymous garage in North London, about ten miles away from Knightsbridge.

'Look, smartass, let's make a deal you won't regret. Listen carefully, all of you. I could leave you handcuffed the way you are now, right? I could also lock this room and, finally, shut the vault door. I could even jam it with a couple of metal paper-clips . . .'

'Please don't,' Digney said in a moaning whisper.

'Let me finish. I said that I could do that but, as I feel that you are smart enough not to push your luck any further, I won't. On the contrary, I am going to free one

valerio viccei

of each of your arms and I won't interfere with the doors. All I want in return is the promise that you won't try to free yourselves before half an hour. Is that understood?'

Parvez replied on behalf of all of them, saying that they wouldn't leave the room until the police came and freed them.

'Anyway, folks, the bad news is that one of my men will be waiting in the control room for some time after I go. If you break our agreement and come out of here when he is still around, he has been instructed to shoot you straightaway. You take your chances.'

They all nodded and I could tell that none of them would ever try to open the door before they were supposed to; I calmly proceeded to undo their handcuffs. I thought of myself as a fair opponent and, as the guards had not given me a hard time at all, I was prepared to take a little risk in order to make them feel more comfortable and relaxed. No winner should ever try to overkill a good loser.

All the others were upstairs, a little concerned about the reason for my delay, but things looked good and at this stage only a stupid mistake on our part could transform success into failure.

I told 4 to wear overalls on top of his clothes. As agreed, he would go out on his own and fetch the van. With the overalls on, he would look like a removal man and this would help to confuse witnesses who might happen to observe the loading operation. He hesitated a little, then reached for the overalls, but I could feel it, something was amiss.

too fast to live

'Any problem, buddy?'

'No, nothing,' he said a little too quickly.

I dug into my trouser pocket and handed him the keys to the van.

'You need just one move to get out of the parking slot, and one more to park it sideways, just opposite this door. Can you do it?'

'Yes, I don't see why not, but . . .' he stuttered like a frightened kid. My spine shivered and I couldn't help thinking that if the son of a bitch became jumpy while at the wheel, he might make a real mess of it. He could easily bump into a parked car which, with my luck, would be protected by some sophisticated alarm system. I could almost hear the high-pitched noise and see everybody in the street turning towards the source of it.

I grabbed the keys back and told him he was a jerk. 2 shook his head, but said nothing; I bet he could read my thoughts. I told him that I was going out again and he was to make sure that the back door didn't lock itself. As soon as I parked the van in front of the door, 3 would come out and act as a security guard, radio in hand. Peter and 4 would start loading the van, while 2 kept the door open. When the last item was loaded, they would all jump into the van; only 4 would leave on foot. I didn't even wait for their comments. I was terribly pissed off and my temper was beginning to get the better of me.

Loading the loot was a swift operation and only a couple of passers-by appeared to pay any attention to what was happening. I kept scanning the street for police but my gut feeling was that now nothing was going to

valerio viccei

interfere with our getaway. 4 was already walking down Cheval Place at a quick pace; in fifty yards he would disappear into Brompton Road.

Everybody was in the back of the van now, the silence unreal, broken only by the creaking of the van's suspension. The weight was so great that the tyres looked dangerously flat to me. I turned the key and the engine started smoothly. My eyes were glued to the side mirrors: nobody in front, nobody behind.

I drove away. Two hundred yards, three hundred . . . still nobody in sight: We had made it! I couldn't resist a scream of joy and my left hand grasped 2's arm. He too smiled and shouted. The atmosphere was one of pure ecstasy: we knew we had written a page of criminal history. We had just pulled off the boldest, largest and most spectacular robbery in recent times.

*   *   *

I drove slowly, paying total attention to the other vehicles around me, a bloody crash was all I needed. Because it was a Sunday, the traffic was bearable. Nevertheless, I decided to avoid crossing Hyde Park and drove straight on instead, towards Kensington High Street. Once I reached the Royal Park Hotel I told the lads to get out of the van and be very careful. They must follow my previous instructions to the letter and leave the country immediately, it didn't matter where for. Once they were on foreign soil their options would be open, but it was imperative that they disappeared before the police were

too fast to live

alerted. It wasn't that any of them would be at any risk of being identified, but I feared that a massive police presence at the airport might panic them and then disaster would strike.

Having dropped them off, I turned right into Church Street and continued my solitary drive filled with a sense of sheer satisfaction; I was on top of the world. I was longing to empty the bags on to the floor of my penthouse and examine their contents.

Very shortly I was in Notting Hill Gate and leaving central London behind me. Even if they discovered what had happened at the Centre right now, I would still easily slip through the police net. London is far too big to be completely sealed off.

In less than ten minutes I was driving along Hampstead High Street; it was 6.00 pm and the sun was well up in a cloudless blue sky. I couldn't afford to relax yet but as the distance separating me from Steve's place grew less and less, my excitement became almost unbearable.

The driveway leading to Steve's block of flats was as quiet as ever — just a few parked cars and a couple walking their little dog. As a matter of routine and instinctive precaution, I automatically scanned the surrounding windows and balconies for anything unusual, but all was calm.

As we agreed, I sounded the horn three times and waited for Steve to appear at the window of his living room. There he was, the turncoat to be, smiling broadly at the sight of the van's flat tyres. My expression must have also given him a clue; the son of a bitch came down in a matter of seconds and didn't hide his joy.

He said nothing, just smiled and walked in front of the van until we reached the garage. Curiosity must have been killing him, but I could hardly blame him because I felt the same myself.

Crazy as it may sound, the fact that I was now a multimillionaire did not play any part in my happiness. I sat at the wheel of the van and relived the most exciting bits of this unforgettable afternoon. The load in the van was simply my reward for success. Money is a tool, an extremely powerful one, but only a tool nevertheless. It gives me self sufficiency and total autonomy from a society in which I have no faith. Luxury and highly expensive toys come with it, of course, as does the good life, but I had been there already over and over again. I had also spent years in the toughest prisons you could think of and survived the punishment blocks endless times. I knew how to enjoy life, but I also knew how to suffer with dignity. It was all part of the same game and I had learned to play by its rules. I am a true predator and predators never cry!

As I explained earlier, the van was far too big for the garage door, therefore I did my best to park it in such a way that the unloading process would appear totally normal to the occasional observer. Steve had gone upstairs to fetch a few cold drinks, but I couldn't wait any longer. I had to get out of the van. I opened the garage door first and then the one on the side of the vehicle. The huge trunks were piled up on my right and I took

too fast to live

the top one and put it on the floor. I walked back to the van and grabbed one of the green bags, but when I tried to lift it I had the shock of my life: I simply couldn't do it! I am quite a strong chap by all standards and on a good day I can bench press over 120 kilos. This bloody thing must have weighed at least 100 kilos!

Thank God, Steve came back at almost the same time and an iced Coke helped to ease my increasing thirst. I told him what had just happened and he could hardly believe it. We both realised that we wouldn't be able to transfer all the stuff inside the trunks, let alone carry them up to the third floor. We were discussing this new problem when a strange noise came from inside the van. We both jumped!

It was the cursed bleeper and hearing it made me look at my watch right away; it was now 18.45 and this meant that the poor bastards were still in the viewing room.

While I headed for the van, I tried to explain to Steve what it was all about. I grabbed a big hammer and hit the bleeper straight on its little speaker. I didn't need it any more; it could rest in peace.

Had I followed my original plan, things would have been a little too elaborate at this point and, considering the way the operation had been carried out, I felt that I could afford to take a few little risks. The little bleeper had just told me that the police still did not know what had happened and we were now about ten miles from Knightsbridge. Even an idiot could work out that the police reaction would be to check vehicles leaving

valerio viccei

London, not the other way round.

Basically, we should now unload the van and put everything inside the trunks, if we could, then padlock them, lock the garage and leave in Steve's BMW and the van. We should ditch the van somewhere in Finchley Road and continue in the car until we reached the West End. Once there, we should hail a taxi and collect the Passat, still parked in Trevor Square, no more than three hundred yards from the Safe Deposit Centre itself! We would then drive all the way back to Steve's garage in both cars, load the Passat with as many trunks as we could, go to Redington Road and carry the load up to the penthouse!

My quick calculations told me that we would need to repeat the whole operation at least three times and then start to sort the stuff. I didn't fancy it much.

On the other hand, I realised that this decision was a very important one and what I would or wouldn't like could play no part in it. I sat down to think for a while. Many factors now had to be taken into account, several of which could not have been considered at the time of planning. First of all, the van was 100% clean; once the plates had been changed, it would be just one of thousands of similar white vans being driven around London. Secondly, the operation had been extremely neat, therefore the police would have nothing to work on for at least a few hours. Thirdly, there was so much stuff that the trunks would need to be loaded and reloaded many times over.

I decided we would split the contents of the green

too fast to live

bags, not only among the trunks but also into the two large suitcases, the pilot-cases and all the spare green bags still unused. This way we would be able to distribute the weight equally and carry the packages up to my flat.

This operation would take place inside the garage, of course. Once completed, we would reload the van with everything apart from the tools. Finally, we would change the Renault van number plates. At this point Steve would take his BMW and I would follow in my vehicle; in less than ten minutes we would be in Redington Road and ready to move the whole lot in one go. Once this had been done, we would leave the flat and ditch the van somewhere. Steve would recover the Passat the following day at his leisure. No problem!

*   *   *

Carrying a dozen bags up to the third floor was bad and carrying the suitcases was even worse, but the trunks nearly killed me. I didn't know what the hell there was in there, but I would never have believed we could get so much stuff out of the boxes.

I lay exhausted on the carpet of my bedroom floor. I did not dare lie on the bed cover; I stank like a pair of unwashed socks and sweat had soaked every single item of my clothing. I was worn out but I couldn't afford to rest, yet. The van was still conspicuously parked in the driveway and I wanted to get rid of it as soon as possible. It was the only thing, apart from my blood and finger-prints, to tie me to the robbery. I told Steve to move his ass and follow me; in a minute we were off again.

*   *   *

A long hot shower did me a lot of good and my energy seemed to have been recharged by the half dozen sandwiches I had just wolfed down. I was wearing a comfortable robe and although there was still a lot to do, I was sitting on the sofa, struggling with the cork of an iced bottle of Krug. The wound on my finger looked a bit nasty and kept bleeding despite the thick dressing, but I decided that I could live with it.

I switched the TV on and tried to relax a little, but there was still a lot to do. My concentration had gone for good and I could no longer think too clearly. It was as if my mind was overloaded. I expected the broadcast to be interrupted at any time and kept changing channels every few seconds. My radio set was also on as was the scanner tuned to police frequencies. It was all noise and confusion but I was completely divorced from my surroundings!

Just a few minutes before Steve left the flat, I told him that I wanted to do something that I had seen in a movie many years ago and which had stayed in my memory since. I wanted to fill the tub in the main bathroom with all the cash.

The money was much more than I had expected it to be. It all was in large denomination bills, neatly packed and in so many different currencies that some of them were totally alien to me. I knew immediately how I would spend that night and probably most of the

too fast to live

following day. I gave Steve five grand and told him to leave: I did not want to share this intimacy with anybody else. I wanted to be alone with the spoils!

To be honest, I was still very much confused and too excited to do anything but relive what had happened in the last five hours. Everything was so out of proportion that I needed to think carefully about my next moves, but in the end I decided that I could afford not to think at all. I would leave that to the police.

The TV and the other media did not come up with anything at all, which struck me as totally out of order as it was now 8.00 pm and surely by this time Knightsbridge must have been taken over by the police. (In actual fact, the news wouldn't be broken by the media for three whole days. It nearly drove me up the wall!)

I couldn't understand it at all at the time and I let tiredness overcome my resistance. I decided to have a quick nap on the sofa to help my brain to recover some of its efficiency; the certainty that my dreams would be as sweet as honey was unshakeable.

I woke very suddenly and a glance at my watch told me that only an hour had gone by since I passed out. The reason for waking was the noise coming from my bleeper and I had to rush and fetch it. 'Just arrived. I will contact you again tomorrow. Best of luck, 3.' The message spoke for itself and I was pleased that once again my plan was working. Only when all of them had sent a similar message, however, would I be in a position to relax.

I did not have to wait too long for another confirmation. This time it was 4. From our previous chats I had

valerio viccei

guessed that he and 3 would move quickly, while the other two might attempt to fly to another continent. If this was the case, I wouldn't hear from them until tomorrow.

All of a sudden the bleeper went off once again. This time the message was from Pamela! She had left a telephone number and the name of a hotel. In the little screen I could also read that she wanted me to call her immediately.

'Hello, may I speak to Miss Seamarks, please?'

'One momento, señor.'

The usual clicking noise of a busy hotel's switchboard followed and I couldn't help thinking that this might mean bad news. Nevertheless I felt that I was safe and I wouldn't let her say a single word on the phone . . .

'Who's speaking?'

'You just called, so you should know.'

'Ohhh, congratulations! He just called me from a box saying that everything went well. I am really glad that you managed it.'

'Yes, thank you, Pam. The land deal was fine and the lawyers did not put up a big fight. I am definitely satisfied with the result.'

'When can I see you?'

'Pam, you must be joking! I am very busy and you are having a break; we also had a very clear agreement, so stick with it.' I replied hardly suppressing my rage and cursing Parvez under my breath.

'I know that, but don't get upset, please. It is only because I am missing you and it is terribly boring here. Is there any possibility that you will leave the country in a few days? Please . . .'

'All right! Look, I will try my best and I will let you know as soon as possible, but you may have to meet me elsewhere as I don't think my business will bring me to Spain. Till then, just keep quiet and please don't call again. I have your number and I shall contact you shortly, OK?'

The call had reminded me that there were still plenty of risks and that the sooner I got rid of the loot, the better! I did not want negative thoughts to spoil this marvellous day and I couldn't think of a more therapeutic distraction than to start sorting part of my treasure. I also needed to have a rough idea of the amount of cash I could count on. I wanted to give £100,000 to each of the lads and three times as much to Parvez and myself. Just over a million!

'Peanuts!' I told myself glancing at the bath tub full of money.

*   *   *

I was aching all over and I had no concept of time and space. I could be dreaming, awake or even dead. All I knew was that I felt extremely tired and that my right arm was throbbing with pain.

I slowly extricated my head from beneath the pillow and tried to focus on my surroundings, but the light was too intense and my optic nerves screamed in pain. This enabled me to register three things: I had been sleeping, I

valerio viccei

wasn't dreaming and I was still alive in my own bed!

I was out of bed in a flash. I couldn't give a damn about the pain, my eyes or any other thing in the world for that matter. I remembered quite clearly what had happened.

I thought that it couldn't be later than 7 am and a quick glance at the night-stand, where only a few hours before I had placed a silver clock with a personal dedication from the royal family on it, confirmed that it was even earlier. The sun had not yet completely risen but its rays were already so powerful that they sneaked through the large gap in the curtains with ease. The carpet of my bedroom floor was entirely covered by a sea of diamonds, rubies, emeralds, sapphires, pearls, gold . . . and every other sort of treasure you could think of. There was so much of it that it would be impossible to walk around without wearing slippers. Those stones looked pretty sharp! On the writing desk, that same desk at which I had spent sleepless, endless nights working on the plan, were the most beautiful pieces of all. No more than fifteen or twenty of them, their value was £20 million at least!

One single diamond was 41 carats, many others were well over 20. Some of the necklaces, with stones the size of a one pound coin, had hundreds of smaller diamonds on them and the sun seemed to be specially attracted by this unique display of nature's pride. As a result, a glittering, almost kaleidoscopic light hit my eyes and my pupils must have shrunk to the size of needle points. I had to reach for my sunglasses!

too fast to live

I didn't want to miss a single second of it. I walked back to the bed and sat down on it, my head resting against a pyramid of pillows. In the middle of the room was a Persian carpet and on this I had piled all the cash; its amount was staggering beyond belief.

I didn't have time to count all of it, but from what I already knew, it came to millions.

Next to me, on the same night-stand where the clock was, sat a solid gold tray on which I had placed a rock of pure cocaine weighing over a kilo.

I reached for the golden tray and snipped a fragment off the huge rock of cocaine. I grabbed a platinum credit card belonging to some asshole with three family names and five titles just to cut myself a line of this beautiful stuff. Then I rolled a 1,000 Swiss franc bank note and zapped it in one go! I lay on my back again and took a long breath of pride and satisfaction. I rested my hands behind my head and said very quietly, 'I did it!

CHAPTER 11

London, a Month Later

Whites Hotel is just a few yards away from Hyde Park. It is small, but very exclusive and its entrance is protected by a low wall. Tourists with cameras milled around trying to find something to snap, a common sight in this part of the Bayswater Road with its endless rows of crowded hotels and restaurants.

Unmarked police cars, discreetly stationed in the area, hid quite unnoticed. The Flying Squad detectives sitting in them seemed relaxed, concentrating mainly on ways of coping with the scorching heat of that sultry August day. They were obviously not there by chance and their attention seemed to be focused on the well-kept, secluded entrance to Whites. The whole team had been specially set up by Scotland Yard to investigate the Safe

valerio viccei

Deposit Centre robbery. The detectives had all been hand-picked and were acting under the supervision of a burly Inspector. His name was 'Fred' Leach and he was a very ambitious cop. All he wanted was the results and he wanted them quickly.

The robbery had been carried out with great determination and efficiency, but without the slightest trace of violence. This, notwithstanding, the pressure had been unbearable and everybody had worked their ass off over the only two pieces of evidence available to them; my fingerprints and bloodstains. Patience, hard work and . . . good luck had finally paid off. When I injured my hand and the glove tore, I left prints all over the vaults; the hounds had picked up the scent and they were now after me.

According to their preliminary guesstimates, the robbery must be worth at least thirty million pounds. Just a very conservative estimate, since hardly any of the victims had co-operated with the investigators.

Famous jewellers, gold and diamond dealers, Greek, Arab and Jewish millionaires, stockbrokers, actors and titled people besieged the Safe Deposit Centre as soon as the media broadcast the news. Their faces, distorted with rage and indignation, were pitilessly preserved for posterity by BBC TV cameras. In the House of Commons, opposition MPs gloated over them, while taxi-drivers and chance passers-by showed both scorn and delight. This robbery would go down in history. Such a thing couldn't have happened to a more deserving lot, to the great pleasure of the less well-off. The box holders were definitely on their own and opinion polls would show that public sympathy was hugely on my side.

It was only a few days since the Scotland Yard men had managed to identify the fingerprints I left in the vaults, amid great surprise and anger! Of course, they had no idea where I was. The last sight of me dated back to about seven months previously . . . when, together with Helle, I left my friends' house in the black cab.

These detectives were now keeping Pinkas under observation. He had gone into Whites with another Israeli for a short while, then left and 'been taken care of' by another surveillance team. Not that Pinkas had any particular significance for them, but his name did appear on the log book of a white Ferrari confiscated by the Extradition Squad after my escape in January. I had repeatedly warned him of that and he knew he should never meet with me unless I made the necessary arrangements. He was never supposed to be at Whites with my buyer. Leach knew that Pinkas could well lead them into a blind alley and along devious trails, but that's all he had to go by for the moment.

My new shining Ferrari Testarossa drew to a halt opposite the main entrance of Whites Hotel. The porter welcomed me attentively and even opened the car door. When I emerged from the car, I must have looked like a well-dressed executive in his thirties who carried the inevitable portable phone and a Vuitton briefcase.

A few words and a laugh passed between me and the porter, the cops must have thought I was one of the wealthy hotel guests telling him to take good care of his

valerio viccei

pet possession. I smiled and quickly leapt up the few steps leading into the hotel lobby. The detectives looked on with a mixture of envy and curiosity. My little toy costs something like £100,000. They couldn't even begin to calculate how many years' salary that would take.

Once Pinkas left the hotel, 'Fred' Leach had decided to make a discreet identity check on all those visiting Whites over the next few hours. Unbeknown to me, I would therefore be checked too. One of the team left his vehicle to perform this task, when I emerged from the front door and took the car keys back from the porter. He clearly didn't know who I was and why I left the hotel so quickly.

Just as I revved up the powerful V12 engine of my Ferrari, the same detective checked up on me with the head of staff. From what he learned, he took no more interest in me than he did in the other guests. He was told that I was a wealthy businessman called Raiman, who was well known in the hotel. I travelled a lot and was not even staying at Whites at the time. He asked if I happened to have an appointment with a couple of foreigners who had just left the hotel, the manager replied that I had indeed!

The detective was taken aback, but it was the answer to his next enquiry which eliminated any doubt. It sent him tearing out of the lobby like an Olympic runner in the 100-metres final.

'Can you tell me if Mr Raiman is also a foreigner?'

'Oh yes . . .' came the reply '. . . he is Italian.'

The detective literally shouted this news to the rest of

too fast to live

the team and, after frantic radio discussions with headquarters, a decision was made by Leach. This implied immediate action. If they had the right man, they couldn't afford to make any more false moves. Nor could they try using me as a decoy to identify the other culprits. Too dangerous a business.

They were pinning their hopes on me being unarmed, as I had managed to escape seven months earlier without producing a weapon. If I was armed it could prove disastrous. Luck was on their side, of course, as I was not carrying my faithful Beretta, but calmly driving through the nightmarish London traffic which, at 1.30 in the afternoon was jammed solid.

The fact that the Israeli I had an appointment with was not at Whites was very strange, but it was Pinkas's unrequested and unplanned presence there that had alerted my senses. Bad vibes, no more than that.

Marble Arch is well known, to those with any experience of London, as a driver's nightmare. A few hundred metres drive took up to one hour and my car was now stuck in the middle of the chaos.

The arrest that followed was not an easy one. I immediately realised that my chances of escape were nonexistent and that my car was being quickly surrounded by plain clothes cops; I had a go. As I accelerated, the Ferrari's large tyres screeched on the melting asphalt and one of the detectives was dragged along for many metres. He had had the very unfortunate idea of trying to grab the ignition key, but was not quick enough. Other Flying Squad officers were already

valerio viccei

blocking the traffic ahead which meant that I had nowhere to go. My various attempts to push other cars out of the way to get through did not work despite my determination. The game was up and I knew it. My windscreen was smashed with an object of some kind and, to the astonishment of passers-by, I was literally dragged through the windscreen. Any resistance would have been pointless and almost comical. Half a dozen cops were all trying to handcuff me at once and not being very kind to me either — not one little bit!

There was not a lot I could say and my only words, later recorded in the log book by DS James Goldie, were, 'Right, chaps, the game is up now and you have no need to be nasty. You are the winners so calm down and everything is going to be fine!'

Paddington Green high security police station is in the Edgware Road just a few hundred metres away, and the trip there was very quick — very quick indeed!

'Mr Raiman, you are in a high security police station now and obviously under arrest. My name is James Goldie and I am the Scotland Yard detective who will be dealing with you at this stage. I already know that your real name is Valerio Viccei, and you are an Italian who is wanted in your own country as well.'

'You have a good sense of humour, Mr Goldie. As a matter of fact, I believed we were at Buckingham Palace and you were my personal bodyguard!' I replied.

'Procedure, I am afraid, and things will be done by the book. You will soon be charged with various offences. Therefore, I want to know if you understand

too fast to live

what I have to say, or if we have to get an interpreter. Just say "yes" or "no" as whatever you say may be used in evidence against you.'

'Apart from your Scottish accent, detective, nothing is wrong with your English. But what about a lawyer?'

'Well, I am pleased that we have no need for an interpreter, but for the time being you will be denied access to a lawyer. Because of the seriousness of the offences you will soon be charged with, my chief has instructed me that you must be held incommunicado. Do you understand this word?'

'No I don't, but I have the feeling that you mean that I will be kept isolated from everybody for some time, uh?'

'More or less . . .'

'Look, Mr Goldie, before you leave you should try to speak again to this chief of yours. It is crystal clear that my position is totally compromised and all I can do for the time being is to keep innocent people out of trouble.'

'Well, Valerio, I am prepared to do so but I need something more specific or he won't pay any attention to what I will say.'

'Right, I am gonna propose him a deal — take it or leave it. So listen carefully to what I want you to tell your boss . . .'

Aftermath

STEPHEN MANN As far as Steve is concerned, he earned the distinguished title of 'supergrass'. He informed on everybody and gave evidence even against people he had never met. He was exposed as a professional liar by the trial judge himself who warned the jury repeatedly about his credibility. He was sentenced to five years. He is now a free and very worried man.

PETER O'DONOHUE I used to like the chap and I trusted him. Once arrested he proved to be very sneaky and did whatever he could to save his own skin. He made devastating statements involving all of us and, in the end, even himself. Ironically enough his most self-damaging statement was dismissed by Judge Lymbery. This bit of

valerio viccei

luck and his refusal to give evidence in court enabled him to get away with a lesser charge and he was sentenced to eleven years. He was the only one who had the chance to avoid arrest but, instead of doing what you would expect, and trying to save part of the loot, he 'stoically' waited for the police, with one difference. He persuaded Helle to provide him with an alibi, which, under the circumstances, was totally out of order. The girl was to say that they had spent that fateful Sunday afternoon in bed together. Well, she was charged, arrested and put in Holloway, but stuck with their story only in order to help him. At the same time the rat was already making a full confession and, obviously, exposing her lie. What a tough guy!

DAVID POOLE No criticism of the way he handled himself. He denied his involvement all along and scientific evidence has proved that his self-incriminating statements had been tampered with by the police. He always denied making them and I have no reason to disbelieve him. Unfortunately his appeal failed and his sixteen-year sentence was upheld by Lord Lane in December 1991. I wish him luck.

ISRAEL PINKAS 'Izzy' was the only one who unwittingly — I emphasise that — led the cops to Whites and, in so doing, sealed my fate for ever. He also made sure not to destroy damning evidence and this proved to be fatal as far as the recovery of property and the arrest of some defendants were concerned. I give him credit that, apart from those mistakes, the man has behaved well and has not informed on any of us. Considering the very marginal role he played in disposing of part of the spoils, he was given an unfairly heavy sentence. He pleaded guilty to handling and receiving and was given ten years, later cut to nine by the Court of Appeal. He will be freed soon and I wish him luck. He has a nice wife and two lovely kids of whom I am still very fond.

PARVEZ LATIF He never stood a chance, but he handled himself disgracefully and his statements to the police were suicidal. Pamela struck the heavier blow to his already untenable defence by withdrawing her support to their concocted story. He is serving eighteen years in a low security prison and, it seems, making the best of it. All notwithstanding I wish him luck.

ERIC RUBIN The man is as good as gold. After he had been on the run for over a year he was arrested in Israel. Although a Russian Jew, he was denied the unwritten Israeli rule that has always made sure that their own are never extradited. He was found guilty on police evidence without the slightest corroboration. He has always professed his innocence. He is a man I am fond of and one who knows the meaning of the words loyalty and honour. Unfortunately though, he is very sick and I don't know if he will ever make it. That is the reason why he was sentenced to only twelve years. He was also found guilty of committing the Coutts robbery in Cavendish

valerio viccei

Square.

NUMBER FOUR Steve Mann and Peter did not know his name or his whereabouts, therefore he was never identified or arrested. I know he is OK.

PAMELA SEAMARKS Pam was arrested following information provided by Steve Mann and the discovery of a damning piece of evidence in Pinkas's flat. The latter consisting of a bill-printout issued by the Hilton Hotel in Tel Aviv, where Pamela and I had been staying just two weeks after the robbery. As for Steve Mann, I personally gave him £50,000 in cash to open a savings account on her behalf: his evidence proved to be fatal.

Following my own arrest, she and Parvez tried to concoct a story where they would both appear the victims of a heartless bandit who used deceit, threats and blackmail to win their co-operation. It backfired very badly. Peter and Steve, in fact, knew exactly what happened and, when they started to sing, the whole game blew up in their faces. Eventually, she pleaded guilty to receiving stolen goods and was sentenced to 18 months, suspended.

For my part, I tried to protect her as best I could — probably more than I did anybody else — and I did so even in court when we all knew that the game was up for good. Despite this, for which I did not expect anything in return, she behaved very badly indeed. I understood the silly and unpleasant lies she decided to tell the police, as she may have acted out of fear and self-preservation, but there is no excuse for what she told the media after the trial was over! She shamefully lied with regard to the nature of our relationship, my behaviour and her role in the whole story. These lies were at the time readily bought by some tabloids for serious money. Then, out of the blue, I received an apologetic letter from her. She asked for understanding and forgiveness, adding that she had had no control over the press and that she had badly needed the money. The letter ended as follows: 'I am sorry for any embarrassment caused, I too had to suffer the words . . . Only we know the real facts so we can laugh inside for ever.'

Strange as it might sound, I do like Pam and I am also pretty fond of her. She was a girl with little experience of real life and a lot to learn about men. Once I got to know her better I discovered a sweet and caring person: her dominant character was only a front. She was weak and insecure. She tried to dominate in order to avoid domination, it is as simple as that. I feel no resentment and I have forgiven her completely for whatever she did and said. I have also accepted her explanation and understood the predicament she found herself in. Her role was totally irrelevant as far as the crime was concerned. I want to make that clear, but she was living with Latif and, at the same time, having a tempestuous relationship with me. I simply couldn't leave her out of the picture.

We have been corresponding regularly since my arrival at Parkhurst and up to six months ago. I have never hidden from her what I was going to write in this book, but when I sent her the excerpts of the two chapters regarding the nature of our relationship, she disappeared. I have not heard from her since and I resent it.

HELLE SKOVBON 'Topino' is the sweetest kid in the world, which doesn't mean she is perfect. Thanks to Peter's brilliant idea she spent a few weeks in prison and earned some reputation. She pleaded guilty to receiving some silly presents from me and was sentenced to three months, all suspended. She is still 'coping' with me and, since the trial, has devoted herself only to two commitments: her work as manageress in a West End boutique and looking after me. My family love her and so does everybody I know. I don't know what the future holds for us, but at the moment she is very important to me and I owe her a lot.

MYSELF I attempted to add an extra chapter explaining many things to this paperback edition of my book. But my publishers were forced to remove this because of the threat of libel action from a police officer who shall remain nameless and . . . shameless! This book should have said it all, but controversy will follow and some of the public will not be prepared to believe what I have stated. I have not tried to portray myself as a modern Robin Hood, nor am I interested in such an image. I am a bank robber and, by society's standards, a dangerous man. I do not glorify crime and I would never advise anybody to follow my painful and risky path. I made the

too fast to live

wrong choice when I was a youngster and, from then onwards, it has been like a snowball effect. Regret plays no part in what I am saying: those emotions belong to myself and to the sleepless nights I have to live with. As for my denigrators and the outrage provoked by what I have finally decided to reveal, a public document produced by the prosecution during the trial is available to them. It is a letter I wrote in Italian during the few days spent in police custody and which I addressed to 'The Magistrate'. I totally ignored the way penal proceedings are dealt with in this country, so I assumed that the continental way would work all the same. Obviously I was wrong, but this letter, although translated in very poor English by a police interpreter, will speak on my behalf and make some people feel ashamed of what they said in the past with regard to my greed and selfishness. Here is EXHIBIT 184 in its original form.

```
Your Worship (the Magistrate),
    I apologise for writing in a foreign
language   which   could   cause
complications but my English is very
elementary and poor that it would be
difficult for me to express my true
opinions.
    My position in this hearing is very
emblematic and easily provable, this
is chiefly thanks to my admissions and
```

valerio viccei

to the accusations of my co-defendants.

<u>I am the person responsible for the entire operation of the 12th July.</u>

I conceived it, planned it, organised it, physically carried it out and finally managed the sales phase. How many others participated in different roles in the main crime or in those closely connected with it will not be identified by me because of an ethical choice and behaviour which shrinks from any personal advantages or daily benefits.

In effect, their responsibilities greatly diminished, in general there was no covetousness of cash, but only emotional and affectionate involvement.

I am not trying to protect anyone but I am pleading with you to get to the heart of my human drama, all the more intense because girls, friends or simply acquaintances found themselves or find themselves in trouble only because they?? or for having accepted a petty gift from yours truly. It was inevitable that such a secret and complex situation should have such complex and hidden consequences but in the excitement/agitation of the events errors of valuation could have been committed which could weigh heavily on the freedom of innocent and alien

too fast to live

individuals. Everything that I have stated will be confirmed by direct and indirect checks, I have never lied, looking at it at it's sic worst I have kept silent.

I beg you to be unbiased and humane in judging the individual cases; it has been for them all an unrepeatable adventure, of something that involved them without their being able to escape and, for my part, you will acknowledge, that none of them can be considered a criminal.

The most significant aspect of the operation, fortunately carried out by the police, which diligently managed and reached more than positive results in a few days, is due to the involvement of some girls — not because of my masculine view of life or because of an exasperated sense of gallantry, but I think, that on their part there is an innate tendency to let oneself be involved in any type of adventure that has as its protagonist the man of the moment, whom they would follow even to hell. In context of the situation I gave some insignificant gifts, I spent my time and travelled with some of them, I also entrusted them with some money, but I assure you on my word of honour and on my deep sense of dignity

valerio viccei

which I will never fail that it was not the money or the profits that they wanted; it just became difficult to say no.

It is the same as when you desperately love someone, sometimes you are willing to accept their betrayals, but this does not mean that we share and accept the matter. What I have done is very serious, I can answer for myself as I answered for myself before, I ?? with society and I will pay with my best years for this, but I do not repudiate my choices, maybe I am a romantic lunatic who lives in his own world of dreams/fantasies, but money was the last thing on my mind. I was always waiting to reach something that was the top of its field, without physical violence and reducing the use of others to the minimum. I am at peace with myself, I have not dragged anyone in the mud, neither have I tried to avoid my responsibilities; if I could be the only one to pay and see all the others free, I would not care the price, but I know this is not possible and so I am trying to suggest to the Court the fairest way to inflict a proportioned individual punishment and not an indiscriminate example of summary justice. The law should not be

too fast to live

afflictive but educational and without vengeance. The criminal is only an erring son of society but always one of its creatures.

> Yours faithfully,
> Valerio Viccei.

Please note: ?? = unable to read the original italian
/ = either word is suitable.